D1212264

WHAT CAN I DO NOW?

WHAT CAN I DO NOW?

Preparing for a Career in Public Safety

Ferguson Publishing Company, Chicago, Illinois

Printed in the United States of America
V-4

Library of Congress Cataloging-in-Publication Data

Preparing for a career in public safety.
    p.   cm. -- (What can I do now?)
    Includes bibliographical references and index.
    Summary: Explores the career opportunities in the field of public safety, provides a detailed look at eight specific occupations, discussing education and training needed, skills required and salary ranges, and offers advice on steps to prepare for a career
    ISBN 0-89434-255-X
    1. Police--Vocational guidance--United States--Juvenile literature. 2. Fire fighters--Vocational guidance--United States--Juvenile literature. 3. Emergency medical services--Vocational guidance--United States--Juvenile literature. [1. Police--Vocational guidance. 2. Fire fighters--Vocational guidance. 3. Emergency medical services--Vocational guidance. 4. Corrections--Vocational guidance. 5. Vocational guidance.]
    I. Series.
HV8143.P74   1998
363.1'0023'73--dc21   98-16380
                                          CIP
                                          AC

Ferguson Publishing Company
200 West Madison, Suite 300
Chicago, Illinois 60606
800-306-9941
www.fergpubco.com

About
the Staff

- Holli Cosgrove, *Editorial Director*
- Andrew Morkes, *Editor*
- Veronica Melnyk, *Assistant Editor*
- Shawna Brynildssen, Veronica Melnyk, Beth Oakes, Elizabeth Taggart, *Writers*
- Connie Rockman, MLS; Alan Wieder, *Bibliographers*
- Patricia Murray, Bonnie Needham, *Proofreaders*
- Joe Grossmann, *Interior Design*
- Parameter Design, *Cover Design*

Contents

Introduction

If you are considering a career in public safety—which presumably you are since you're reading this book—you must realize that the better informed you are from the start, the better your chances of having a successful, satisfying career.

There is absolutely no reason to wait until you get out of high school to "get serious" about a career. That doesn't mean you have to make a firm, undying commitment right now. Gasp! Indeed, one of the biggest fears most people face at some point (sometimes more than once) is choosing the right career. Frankly, many people don't "choose" at all. They take a job because they need one, and all of a sudden ten years have gone by and they wonder why they're stuck doing something they hate. Don't be one of those people! You have the opportunity right now—while you're still in high school and still relatively unencumbered with major adult responsibilities—to explore, to experience, to try out a work path. Or several paths if you're one of those overachieving types. Wouldn't you really rather find out sooner than later that you're not cut out to be an FBI agent after all, that you'd actually prefer to be a political scientist? Or a corrections officer?

There are many ways to explore the field of public safety. What we've tried to do in this book is give you an idea of some of your options. The chapter "What Do I Need to Know about Public Safety?" will give you an overview of the field—a little history, where it's at today, and promises of the future; as well as a breakdown of its structure—how it's organized—and a glimpse of some of its many career options.

The "What Do I Need to Know about Careers?" section includes eight chapters, each describing in detail a specific public safety career: border patrol officer, corrections officer, crime analyst, emergency medical technician, FBI agent, fire fighter, police officer, and secret service special agent. These chapters rely heavily on first-hand accounts from real people on the job. They'll tell you what skills you need, what personal qualities you have to have, what the ups and downs of the jobs are. You'll also find out about educational requirements—including specific high school and college classes—advancement possibilities, related jobs, salary ranges, and the employment outlook.

The real meat of the book is in the section called "What Can I Do Right Now?" This is where you get busy and DO SOMETHING. The chapter "Get Involved" will clue you in on the obvious—volunteering and interning—and the not-so-obvious—summer camps and summer college study, high school clubs, and student organizations. In keeping with the secondary theme of this book (the primary theme, for those of you who still don't get it, is "You can do something now"), "Get Involved" also urges you to take charge and start your own programs and activities where none exist—school, community, or even national. Why not?

While we think the best way to explore public safety is to jump right in and start doing it, there are plenty of other ways to get into the public safety mind-set. "Surf the Web" offers you a short, annotated list of Web sites where you can explore everything from job listings (start getting an idea of what employers are looking for now) to educational and certification requirements to on-the-job accounts from those who keep the public safe.

"Read a Book" is an annotated bibliography of books (some new, some old) and periodicals. If you're even remotely considering a career in public safety, reading a few books and checking out a few magazines is the easiest thing you can do. Don't stop with our list. Ask your librarian to point you to more materials. Keep reading!

"Ask for Money" is a sampling of public safety scholarships. You need to be familiar with these because you're going to need money for school. You have to actively pursue scholarships; no one is going to come up to you one day and present you with a check because you're such a wonderful student. Applying for scholarships is work. It takes effort. And it must be done right and often as much as a year in advance of when you need the money.

"Look to the Pros" is the final chapter. It lists professional organizations you can turn to for more information about accredited schools, education requirements, career descriptions, salary information, job listings, scholarships, and more. Once you become a student in the public safety field, you'll be able to join many of these. Time after time, professionals say that membership and active participation in a professional organization is one of the best ways to network (make valuable contacts) and gain recognition in your field.

High school can be a lot of fun. There are dances and football games; maybe you're in band or play a sport. Great! Maybe you hate school and are just biding your time until you graduate. Too bad. Whoever you are, take a minute and try to imagine your life five years from now. Ten years from now. Where will you be? What will you be doing? Whether you realize it or not, how you choose to spend your time now—studying, playing, watching TV, working at a fast food restaurant, hanging out, whatever—will have an impact on your future. Take a look at how you're spending your time now and ask yourself, "Where is this getting me?" If you can't come up with an answer, it's probably "nowhere." The choice is yours. No one is going to take you by the hand and lead you in the "right" direction. It's up to you. It's your life. You can do something about it right now!

Section 1

What Do I Need to Know About

Public Safety

?

Turn your television on

right now, flip through the channels, and chances are you'll see at least one show featuring police officers, firefighters, criminal profilers, or federal investigators. The abundance of these programs reveals our national fascination with the people who devote their careers to keeping the rest of us safe from harm. Maybe you've watched lots of these shows and are pretty sure you've got a handle on what the field of public safety is all about.

Well, think again. The career possibilities are much more complex and—in many instances—exciting than what you'll see portrayed on television. In the real world of public safety, you'll discover jobs that you didn't even know existed. You'll also find that "tough guy" stereotypes of these workers are shattered. There are disabled police officers, sentimental border patrol guards, giggly crime analysts, petite women working as corrections officers, and firefighters with master's degrees in English.

Certain things, however, hold true across the board: All of the careers described in this book require street smarts, creativity, deep-rooted concern for humankind, and tolerance for some degree of physical danger. Many of these jobs hire people straight out of high school and conduct their own training programs or academies. Other jobs are ideal for students who plan on going to college and doing internships in the summer. Others require a two-year associate's degree. Most important of all is that you can get involved in these jobs while you're still in high school. This book will give you a window into the many things you can do to start pursuing your career—right now.

GENERAL INFORMATION

Virtually every aspect of your life involves policies, regulations, and laws that help to promote public safety. Think about it. The exterior of your house meets certain codes, or rules, so that it won't catch on fire easily. Every time you drive a car, you follow a number of rules so that you won't cause or get in an accident. Even your dog has to obey regulations, like leash laws.

GENERAL INFORMATION, CONTINUED

Some people make the mistake of thinking of public safety and the rules that go with it as strictly modern-day concerns. They romanticize the past as a safer, gentler, lawless era. But the fact is that the protection of a group of people—from both outside and inside the group—has been a concern for a long time. You have to look back at our earliest societies' efforts at public safety to truly understand and appreciate where we are today. As these societies developed, it became clear that people would run wild unless certain rules of conduct were created. Some laws evolved from the common agreement of the group's members, while others were handed down by the group's leaders.

But making a law is not the same thing as enforcing it, and soon after the establishment of rules and laws, methods of enforcement sprang up. For a long time, enforcement simply meant punishment. Those who broke the laws were often ostracized or exiled from the group, subjected to corporal punishment, tortured, maimed, or even killed. Enforcement of the law was usually left up to the society's leaders or rulers, often through the soldiers who served in their armies. Often these armies also collected taxes from the population, which were used to maintain the army (and sometimes to line the ruler's pockets).

Eventually, more organized methods of public safety were developed. In England, for example, earlier law enforcement officials were considered servants of feudal lords, kings, and other rulers, and their duties revolved around protecting their masters' interests rather than ensuring the public safety. The more modern law enforcement officials, however, became directly responsible for protecting the people from crime and fire. In addition, they continued to collect taxes, and they were often responsible for the maintenance and safety of public buildings, property, and other facilities. Colonial America followed in England's footsteps and adopted its system of law enforcement.

Cities grew larger during the eighteenth and the nineteenth centuries, and the need arose for even more organized efforts. You can compare the situation to today's urban problems; larger cities often mean more crime, riots, and other disorders. The first modern police force was formed in 1829 in London.

Books and Movies about Public Safety

Books:

Hard Evidence: Detectives Inside the FBI Crime Lab *by David Fisher*

Boot: An LAPD Officer's Rookie Year *by William C. Dunn*

Prisons and the American Conscience: A History of U.S. Federal Corrections *by Paul W. Keve*

Cops: Their Lives in Their Own Words *by Mark Baker*

Young Men and Fire *by Norman MacLean*

Movies:

Backdraft

The Fugitive

The Thin Blue Line

The Border

In the Line of Fire

Fast Fact

Cities in the United States organized police forces as well, beginning with New York in 1844. As the United States stretched across the continent, many states created state police forces to work with those in the cities and towns. Interstate crimes were placed under federal authority, and various agencies, including the U.S. Marshals Office, the Federal Bureau of Investigation, the Secret Service, the Internal Revenue Service, and the Customs Service, were formed to enforce laws across various jurisdictions.

The punishment of criminals changed as well. Beginning in the eighteenth century, efforts were made to create punishments that were equal to the crime. To deter people from committing crimes, societies began to develop specific punishments for specific crimes. These newer penalties generally called for a period of incarceration. Jails and prisons, which had historically been used as temporary holding pens before more permanent punishments like exile or death, became an important feature of these new ideas of punishment. The new prisons hired guards to watch over the prisoners, bring them food, and prevent them from escaping. The first American jails appeared in the late eighteenth and early nineteenth centuries.

Another feature of protecting the public safety was the detection, prevention, and solving of crimes. Police officers who specialized in these efforts became known as detectives. Much like today, their job was to examine evidence relating to a crime in an effort to catch the person or persons responsible. They were also vigilant in trying to prevent crimes or to catch criminals in the act. During the nineteenth century, the first private detectives and detective agencies appeared. These agencies not only worked to solve crimes against their clients, but also offered guard services for people and their property. Solving crimes also became more and more scientific. As early as 1780, a crime was solved when a suspected criminal's shoes were found to match footprints left at the scene of the crime. Toward the end of the nineteenth and the beginning of the twentieth centuries, modern forensic science techniques were developed. Methods were developed to link fingerprints, bullets and other weapons, hair, soil, and other physical evidence found at a crime scene to the crime and the criminal. Laboratories were constructed that were devoted to this work. The Federal Bureau of Investigation's laboratory, established in the 1920s, became the largest and most famed crime laboratory in the world.

Intelligence operations, that is, the collection and evaluation of information about one's rivals or enemies, have also been a part of our history for a

GENERAL INFORMATION, CONTINUED

long time. Spies were often sent from one group into another, to determine each other's strengths and weaknesses. By gaining information about their enemies, groups were better able to protect themselves from attack. Before long, government agencies began to use intelligence-gathering techniques. The Central Intelligence Agency became responsible for preserving the United States' international interests. The FBI was charged with maintaining the country's internal security. Each branch of the military services also operates intelligence forces. The many agencies often work together and with state and local law enforcement officials in preventing and solving crimes and other threats to the public safety.

Preserving and protecting people's safety—especially during emergency situations—extends beyond law enforcement. A major threat to safety has always been fire, and throughout history, people have worked together to protect themselves and their property from fire damage. When a fire broke out, volunteers used to form lines to pass water buckets to douse the fire. In 1736, Benjamin Franklin (1706-1790) organized the first permanent fire brigade in Philadelphia. Many other cities soon began their own fire departments.

Fast Fact

A fugitive spends an average of five years on the FBI's Ten Most Wanted List. Ninety percent of those who've appeared on the list have eventually been caught.

The industrial revolution brought more sophisticated equipment to fighting fires. Nevertheless, when a fire broke out in a city, the results were often devastating because of crowded conditions, poor building techniques, and inadequate water supplies. The Great Chicago Fire of 1871, for example, destroyed much of the city. Codes and regulations were eventually established for buildings that made them less likely to catch fire and spread the fire to other buildings. New techniques and tools like hydrants, extinguishers, and sprinkler systems made it easier to respond more quickly and effectively. Firefighters became highly trained and also skilled in emergency medical techniques.

Emergency medical technicians (EMTs) also began to play an integral role in public safety. In the past, people had to rely on their family, neighbors, and, if they were lucky, the town physician for prompt medical help during an emergency. Now EMTs working for both public agencies and private companies can respond in minutes to critical medical situations as varied as a car accident, a heart attack, and a premature baby's delivery.

Clearly, emergency and protective services involve the cooperation of almost everyone in a society. Politicians draft legislation intended to promote the public well-being and to prevent threats to individual and public safety.

Many organizations, both governmental and private, act as inspectors and watchdogs to see that regulations and laws are obeyed. Industries are always concerned about the safety of both their employees and the products they make. Start paying attention to all of the rules and policies that help to keep you safe. In your home, your workplace, your streets, state, and country, you'll find innumerable measures that ensure your safety and well-being.

"Our motto isn't 'Take Back the Streets.' It's 'Don't lose the streets to begin with.' "—Tommy Sexton, Chief of Police in Mount Pleasant, South Carolina

STRUCTURE OF THE INDUSTRY

By far, the greatest number of people in emergency and protective services are working at the local level. Almost every community has its own police department. In the smallest communities, a police department may have as few as one or two employees. In larger cities, the members of a police department may be divided into many divisions, each with its own area of the city to patrol. A police force may have specialized divisions, such as a Narcotics Squad to combat illegal drugs; a Vice Squad to fight rape, prostitution, and related crimes; a SWAT team that can be called upon in emergency situations; a Hostage Rescue team; and a Bomb Squad. Most police departments employ a military-style ranking system. Patrol officers may become detectives. Police officers may rise through the ranks to become sergeants, lieutenants, or even the Chief of Police for a community. Many other people provide support for a police department, from traffic and police clerks to forensic experts and polygraph examiners.

Other important areas of local law enforcement are probation and parole services. Probation officers are generally attached to the court system, while parole officers work with the correctional system. Both work in cooperation with the police department.

Sheriff departments generally operate at the county level, and provide additional law enforcement efforts among the many communities in a single county. Almost every state operates its own state police department. They are often called "highway patrols" because one of their major responsibilities is to ensure the safety of the highways linking communities.

The U.S. Marshals service, part of the United States Department of Justice, is concerned with crimes that cross state lines. Interstate crimes, as they are called, may involve the transport of stolen vehicles and goods from one state to another. U.S. Marshals are responsible for tracking down wanted criminals and transporting prisoners. They also operate the Federal Witness Security Program and provide security for federal courts and judges.

> **//For the police, more than any other segment of society or government, the rule of law must always remain sacrosanct."—Louis Freeh, Director of the FBI**

Enforcement of federal laws is largely the responsibility of the Federal Bureau of Investigation. The FBI oversees nearly three hundred separate violations, including such federal crimes as kidnapping. A principal duty of the FBI is to investigate people and groups that might pose a threat to the internal security of the country. The Central Intelligence Agency is primarily concerned with matters of international security, monitoring world events as they relate to the safety and interests of the United States.

There are many other agencies operating at the federal level, including the Drug Enforcement Agency, the Secret Service, the Customs Service, the Immigration and Naturalization Service, and the Internal Revenue Service. Each agency oversees a particular jurisdiction, or responsibility, of the law. However, every agency provides support and cooperation to the others, and often work with state and local law enforcement agencies when investigating crimes and apprehending criminals.

The incarceration and rehabilitation of suspected and convicted criminals also occurs at each of the local, state, and federal levels. Communities usually operate jails, which provide temporary housing for people awaiting trial or for convicted criminals awaiting sentencing to permanent prisons. The prison system operates minimum, medium, and maximum security prisons, depending on the nature of the criminal and the crime. Special prisons house mentally ill prisoners or juvenile offenders. People convicted of federal crimes are generally sent to prisons operated by the federal government.

In addition to their most obvious responsibility of fighting fires, fire departments are often charged with the inspection of public and private facilities to ensure that fire codes are enforced. Fire department officials also investigate the causes of fires. Many private individuals and companies are also involved in fire prevention and protection efforts. People are specially trained for the planning, designing, installing, and maintenance of fire safety systems. Others work for insurance companies and ratings bureaus, evaluating and inspecting a building's fire protection, prevention, and resistance capabilities.

Emergency medical technicians (EMTs) are usually the first to respond to emergency situations. Whether employed by a hospital, police department, fire department, or private ambulance company, the EMT crew functions as a traveling arm of the emergency room. An EMT could be called out for virtually any situation that could be described as a medical crisis.

Security agencies and detective agencies work to ensure the public safety as well. Many provide such services as bodyguards, security systems, armed security guards, and private investigation services in order to prevent crimes against people and property. Many private companies also work within the correctional system, operating prisons, providing corrections officers, and other services. Some private companies also provide police and fire services for universities, airports, communities, and many large government facilities and installations.

CAREERS

There are literally hundreds of career options in the field of emergency and protective services. Below are descriptions of a handful of career possibilities, some of which will be explored in greater detail later in this book.

Police officers are responsible for protecting life and property in their community. They preserve the peace, prevent criminal acts, enforce the law, and arrest people who violate the law. Police officers are also charged with enforcing traffic regulations, directing traffic, and providing security and crowd control functions at public events. *State police officers* perform similar duties at the state level, and also enforce the laws and regulations governing the use of highways. Police officers are often confronted with dangerous situations, and must have maturity, bravery, emotional control, and the ability to think clearly and act quickly in times of stress.

Detectives are police officers who almost always work in plainclothes. They are responsible for investigating crimes, pursuing suspects, and building evidence to convict people who have committed crimes. *Private detectives,* also called *private investigators,* investigate crimes and provide security services for businesses and individuals. They are employed by private companies, but often cooperate with government law enforcement officials.

Corrections officers may be employed by local, state, and federal governments. They guard people who have been arrested and are awaiting trial, and people who have been convicted of a crime. Corrections officers are often in contact with dangerous persons, and must be on the alert for disturbances and violence against themselves and other prisoners.

Crime analysts analyze patterns in criminal behavior—attempting to predict their patterns and discern their motives—in order to catch criminals, and improve law enforcement response times. *Crime scene evidence technicians* collect and photograph relevant evidence, such as fingerprints, hairs, and bullets, at a crime scene. *Criminalists* scientifically analyze, compare, and evaluate physical evidence in the laboratory. They may perform autopsies to determine the cause of a person's death, or analyze fingerprints, hair, fibers, blood, and other evidence discovered at a crime scene. *Criminologists* study and research crime from a sociological perspective. They usually work in a university setting rather than for a law enforcement agency. *Forensic psychologists* use criminal evidence or behavior patterns to make a psychological analysis of a criminal and his or her motivations.

Fast Facts

The typical police officer today faces 11.5 times as many violent crimes as his or her counterpart did 25 years ago.

Polygraph examiners administer lie detection tests for local, state, and government agencies, as well as for private businesses. They are specially trained in operating polygraph equipment and in interpreting the results.

Deputy U.S. marshals report to the U.S. attorney general as part of the Department of Justice. Their responsibilities include providing security for the courts, including the judges and other officials, jurors, and witnesses. They also serve warrants and process documents, locate and arrest fugitives, transport prisoners, and manage the Federal Witness Security Program.

FBI special agents investigate violations of over 270 federal laws and operate intelligence activities relating to domestic security matters. Employees of the FBI also work in the bureau's laboratory in Washington, DC, and maintain the world's largest fingerprint identification program. Special agents are also employed by the Secret Service and other branches of federal law enforcement.

Intelligence officers are federal employees who gather, analyze, and report information about the activities of domestic and international groups, and governments of foreign countries, in order to protect the interests and security of the United States. Intelligence officers may be either *case officers*, who work in the field and most often overseas, and *analysts*, who examine information, and who are generally located in offices in and around Washington, DC. Intelligence officers work for the Central Intelligence Agency, the National Security Agency, and for each branch of the Armed Forces. Intelligence officers and FBI special agents must meet particularly rigid educational, physical, and emotional requirements.

Customs officials are employed by the Customs Service, a branch of the Treasury Department. They enforce laws governing the import and export of products, as well as laws against smuggling and revenue fraud. Customs officials collect tariffs, or duties, on products brought into the United States.

Border patrol officers are also federal employees. As part of the Immigration and Naturalization Service of the U.S. Justice Department, they patrol the borders the United States shares with Canada and Mexico to ensure that people do not enter the country illegally and to prevent the smuggling of illegal drugs. Border patrol officers are also stationed at airports and other points of entry, where they check the passports and visas of everyone who enters the country.

Cryptographic technicians are employed by government intelligence agencies, but also by private businesses such as banks. They specialize in coding and decoding messages, documents, and other communications so that their contents remain secret.

Firefighters are generally employees of local governments. They protect people and property from fires and other emergencies by fighting fires, rescuing people trapped or injured by fires or other accidents. They also provide education on fire safety, inspect and enforce fire safety codes and regulations, and investigate the causes of fires. Fire departments often provide emergency

The Truth About Polygraphs

During the 1920s and 1930s, it was discovered that certain physical processes, such as heart rate, breathing rate, and perspiration rate, responded to stress and could therefore be used to detect whether a person was lying. Special machines, called polygraphs or lie detectors, were constructed that could measure these processes while a suspected criminal was being questioned. Polygraphs can also be used to screen out unreliable people from sensitive positions and have been adopted by many private companies and government agencies when hiring new employees.

ambulance and medical services. Firefighters are in constant danger of injury; they must be courageous, physically strong, and able to work as part of a carefully coordinated team.

Emergency medical technicians (EMTs) give immediate first aid treatment to sick or injured persons both at the scene and en route to the hospital or other medical facility. Many EMTs work for private ambulance services. Others are in municipal fire, police, or rescue departments, while a few work in hospitals and medical centers. Also, there are many who volunteer, particularly in more rural areas, where there often are no paid EMTs at all.

> **//One thing about this work, I've seen some beautiful sunrises and sunsets over the years." — Jack Pool, border patrol agent on U.S.-Mexico border for twenty-five years.**

Private security services are provided by *security consultants, security guards,* and *bodyguards.* Generally, these people work as part of companies providing security services to a range of businesses, individuals, and public and private facilities. Security consultants help businesses establish systems to protect their property, employees, and information. Security systems often include security guards, who are stationed at both public and private buildings and facilities. Bodyguards provide individual protection services for executives, politicians, celebrities, and others who desire privacy and safety.

Secret service special agents employed by the Secret Service provide protection for politicians and political candidates—especially the President of the United States—and their families.

Emergency and protective service careers offer opportunities to serve your community and to help offers. Usually, these jobs also offer wide-ranging responsibilities, excitement, opportunities for advancement, and some exposure to dangerous situations. No matter what your personality type or temperament, there are careers in this field that will suit you.

EMPLOYMENT OPPORTUNITIES

As you've probably already figured out, employment opportunities in this field are quite diverse. You could work for a local agency or department, a state organization, or a federal agency like the FBI or the U.S. Department of Immigration and Naturalization. (See the "What Do I Need to Know about Careers?" section for a rundown of some of the local, state, federal, and private agencies and companies.)

Most careers in emergency and protective services have clear-cut entry requirements. These range from requirements for a high school diploma for police officers, to bachelor's and even advanced degrees for special agents and intelligence officers. Certain law enforcement positions require highly specialized scientific knowledge. Some employers also require several years of related work experience, while others (such as the FBI) have a specific age range for hiring. The application process for some of these jobs is notoriously thorough and time-consuming, but don't be discouraged by the paperwork. If you're the kind of person who has a strong sense of responsibility and a commitment to ensuring the well-being of others, you're halfway there.

INDUSTRY OUTLOOK

Careers in emergency and protective services are among the fastest growing in the United States today. Increases in crime rates, and especially increases in public anxiety over crime, have led to demands for heightened law enforcement efforts, tougher sentencing laws, and dramatic increases in the security services industry. Since 1990, several incidents have raised concern over domestic security, particularly the threat of terrorist attacks. The bombing of the World Trade Center in New York in 1993 and the bombing at the Alfred Murrah Federal Building in Oklahoma City in 1995 have caused an increase in domestic intelligence and investigative operations. The "war on drugs" begun during the 1980s created a need for larger numbers of law enforcement officials trained and dedicated to reducing levels of drug trafficking. In the mid-1990s, President Clinton passed new tough-on-crime legislation that increased the numbers of police officers employed at the local, state, and federal levels.

The corrections industry has recorded an increase of nearly 80 percent in the number of prisoners in the last decade. The war on drugs has had an especially great impact on the numbers of people being sent to prison. Public outrage at the early release of many violent criminals has led to demands for legislation ensuring these criminals serve the full length of their sentences. More prisons are being built to accommodate them, and more corrections offi-

OUTLOOK, CONTINUED

cers are being hired to guard them. At the same time, the overcrowding of many correctional facilities has stimulated pressure for more liberal probation and parole efforts, requiring greater numbers of parole and probation officers.

Immigration and customs officials have seen huge increases in the numbers of people and goods, especially drugs, entering the country illegally. Illegal immigration has become an area of national concern as more and more people have entered the country without the required visas and work permits. Crackdowns on illegal immigration have led to increased numbers of border patrol officers and immigration officials to patrol not only the country's borders, but to seek out illegal immigrants in communities across the United States. Employment of border patrol officers, immigration officials, and customs officials remains largely unaffected by changes in the economy.

Intelligence activities remain an important element of government, despite the ending of the Cold War. The breakup of the Soviet Union has created new political situations and instabilities that must be continually monitored and analyzed for their effect on the interests and security of the United States. Terrorist attacks of U.S. targets overseas continue, and a primary function of the country's intelligence agencies is to identify, intercept, and pursue terrorists who seek to harm the country, its citizens, and allies.

Private security activities have been stepped up, especially as many U.S. companies have begun to compete in a global economy. An especially fast-growing area of corporate security is in computer technology, as computers and computer transmissions of information have become more commonplace across the variety of industries.

Fast Facts

Over $20 billion per year in tax dollars is spent on the U.S. correctional system, with most going into the construction, renovation, and staffing of prisons.

Unlike law enforcement careers, employment of firefighters will remain relatively stable over the next decade. However, because they perform such a vital function in ensuring public safety, it's unlikely that their numbers will decrease. In addition, as smaller communities grow, they will probably organize their own permanent fire departments.

Employment statistics favor emergency medical technicians. Currently, the demand for these professionals exceeds the number of people who are trained to do the work. As the general population grows, the need for more medical personnel is increasing, particularly in larger, metropolitan communities.

What Do I Need to Know About

Careers

?

public safety

Border Patrol Officer

SUMMARY

DEFINITION
Border patrol officers *patrol more than eight thousand miles of U.S. border and are responsible for detecting and preventing smuggling and illegal entry of aliens into the United States.*

ALTERNATIVE JOB TITLES
Border patrol guard or agent

SALARY RANGE
$34,000 to $43,000 to $67,000

EDUCATIONAL REQUIREMENTS
High school diploma

CERTIFICATION OR TRAINING
Border patrol training academy

EMPLOYMENT OUTLOOK
Faster than the average

HIGH SCHOOL SUBJECTS
Foreign language (Spanish)
Geography/Social studies
Government
Law
Physical education

PERSONAL INTERESTS
Camping/Hiking
Exercise/Personal fitness
Helping people: protection
Student government

The sky is inky black, with only a sliver of moon casting a faint glow on Bob Mott as he walks alongside miles of fencing. He kicks his boot into the soil now and again and crouches down to take a closer look at the ground. The agent who just finished her shift had reported some suspicious activity in the area, so Bob is checking to see if any new holes have been dug under the fence.

Tonight, he's been assigned to patrol a deep, brushy canyon that has seen an increased flow of illegal alien traffic. He pauses at every bush, tree, and crevice where someone might try to hide. The rest of his shift will be a waiting game. If the night-vision scope operators see anyone on foot or if an electronic sensor detects motion, he'll respond to those areas.

Out of the corner of his eye, he notices the leaves of a nearby shrub flutter in the windless night. He pushes aside a branch and sees the scuffed shoes first, then shines his flashlight beam into the nervous eyes of a Mexican man. Bob asks the man a few questions in Spanish and looks at the obviously forged identification card, then arrests the man. Later, officers at the station will confirm that the man made his way illegally across the border into California. But by that time Bob is back in the canyon, checking more miles of fence line.

WHAT DOES A BORDER PATROL OFFICER DO?

When someone from another country wants to work, study, or vacation in the United States, they have to apply for a special visa to do so. And if they want to move here permanently, they must apply for citizenship. However, many people attempt to cross the U.S. border without a visa—and that's where border patrol officers enter the picture.

Border patrol officers are hired by the Immigration and Naturalization Service (INS) of the U.S. Justice Department to serve as the nation's gatekeepers by enforcing immigrations and customs laws. One of their major activities is patrolling the border to prevent the illegal entry of aliens and to arrest or deport those who attempt to enter. There are officers stationed at every border entry point in the United States, but most heavily along the Mexican border in Arizona, California, New Mexico, and Texas. At these regular crossings, border patrol officers check all cars for people or items hidden in the vehicle. Deciding which cars to stop is almost an art form for border patrol officers. A car that is moving erratically or riding low to the ground could be a sign that it is loaded down with people. Border patrol officers also become experts at spotting a false identification card almost instantly or discerning a tourist from an illegal alien by asking a single question. Officers are authorized to arrest and take into custody illegal aliens or people they suspect of smuggling.

But most illegal aliens don't attempt to cross into the United States at the official borders. Instead, they wait until nightfall and then try to cross in isolated areas where they hope to go undetected. That's why border patrol officers actually perform a great deal of their work in rugged and uninhabited mountains, canyons, deserts, and waterways. Border patrol officers have become known throughout the law enforcement community for their excellent tracking skills, language skills, wilderness survival skills, and their twenty-four-hour availability. In certain areas, the officers even travel by horseback, jeep, mountain bike, and helicopter, using special techniques and equipment such

Lingo to Learn

Coyote: *Slang term for an alien smuggler.*

Jeep-Plane team: *Teams that coordinate aerial surveillance with ground operations, so that wide expanses of border can be covered.*

Linewatch: *A routine activity in which officers patrol the border for would-be crossers and apprehend them.*

Muster room: *A large room where border patrol officers gather to get information and assignments at the beginning of a shift.*

OTM: *This acronym stand for "Other Than Mexican." Aliens are classified as Mexican or OTM.*

Sign cutting: *A technique in which officers smooth the surface of sandy areas along areas used for illegal entries. When these sand traps are examined, they show footprints. Officers can follow the "signs" and apprehend the aliens.*

Stillwatch: *An officer sits and watches a specific area in order to deter any would-be crossers.*

as electronic sensors, night-vision goggles, and other covert surveillance devices.

Border patrol officers also canvas known pickup and drop-off points for illegal aliens and smugglers. For instance, they might check a small town's convenience store, where a phone booth has been used previously for calls to a professional smuggler. Or they might check out an area where piles of clothing and food supplies have been found.

Another part of their work involves assisting other federal and local law enforcement agencies in stopping the flow of drugs and other contraband from being smuggled into the United States. Border patrol officers enforce the customs laws that regulate materials, crops, and goods that enter the country. In recent years, the increase in drug traffic from Central and South America has had a major impact on the duties of border patrol officers. Currently, the prevention of drug smuggling is a large part of the job—and a dangerous part as well. Armed encounters between professional smugglers and border patrol officers have increased markedly, especially in certain sectors of the Mexico-United States border. Because of the risks involved, all officers are specially trained in the use of weaponry. At some border crossings in Arizona and Southern California where officers have been shot at, injured, and even killed by smugglers, the officers now wear bulletproof vests and carry automatic weapons.

WHAT IS IT LIKE TO BE A BORDER PATROL OFFICER?

For the past eleven years, Bob Mott has patrolled the border along the San Diego sector between the United States and Mexico. He says that back in high school, the possibility of joining the Border Patrol never entered his mind. After completing military training and a tour of duty with the U.S. Coast Guard, a family friend who worked as a Border Patrol Supervisor suggested that Bob would be a good candidate for the position. Now, at thirty-four years old, he can't imagine being in any other career.

Bob works one of three shifts, which run from either 7 AM to 3 PM, 3 PM to 11 PM, or 11 PM to 7 AM. On a typical shift, Bob meets in the "muster room" with all of the other officers coming on duty. Here, he'll receive information from the off-going officers about special problems or alien foot traffic patterns that have occurred. "We're also briefed on special 'look-outs'—criminals wanted by federal, state, and local law enforcement agencies who are suspected of being in the border area or trying to escape to Mexico," says Bob. This is also the time when officers are given their location assignments for the shift. When all that business is done, the officers "break muster" and head out to their areas.

The location of Bob's assignment can range from city streets to farmland to deep canyons. "Currently, my sector is involved in something called Operation Gatekeeper, in which we're trying to maintain a high profile to deter aliens from even attempting to cross the border," he explains. Once he arrives at his post, he'll walk up and down the border, watching for any movement or unusual activity. On a typical assignment, Bob will be solely responsible for covering about five miles of border.

"The working conditions are actually one of the best things about this job," Bob says. "I spend very little time behind a desk and get to work with little supervision." Officers in the Chula Vista Border Patrol Station are generally sent out to work alone. One exception is what's called the Police Department Transport Unit, in which two officers assist local police agencies in situations that may involve illegal aliens. "Often, we're called in to serve as skilled translators," notes Bob. Officers will also work as a team when there are trainees assigned to the station, and a senior border patrol officer takes the new officer under his or her wing for on-the-job training.

Bob describes the downside of the job as being the long hours—typically ten-hour shifts, five days a week—with shifts changing every six weeks. "An officer will more likely than not be working on holidays," he says. "This takes away from time with families, which is tough."

During the course of a shift, he may arrest a number of illegal aliens or the border area he's covering may be quiet. When he apprehends an illegal alien, he'll question the person to determine his or her citizenship and immigration status, and then write up an arrest report. After that, he calls for a transport unit to pick the person up and take him or her to the Chula Vista station. "At the station, every person who is

Mountain-Bike Patrols

Would you believe that the latest tool for enforcing immigration laws might be sitting in your garage? Here's a clue: it's got two wheels, eighteen gears, and shock absorbers.

Recently, the Border Patrol launched a three-person mountain-bike division, responsible for patrolling a stretch of border along southern Arizona's Buenos Aires National Wildlife Refuge. In the past, this sprawling and rugged terrain was nearly impossible to defend from the onslaught of illegal immigrants and drug smugglers. The rumble of a sport utility vehicle could be heard for miles, blowing the cover of the officers.

Now the Border Patrol has equipped its officers with Specialized Stumpjumpers to silently scout the region. Armed with powerful night-vision goggles, the officers have been extremely effective. In a single night in 1996, they intercepted 476 pounds of marijuana and sixty illegal immigrants.

Source: **Outside Magazine,** *September 1997*

apprehended is electronically fingerprinted, and their fingerprints are compared against a database," Bob explains. "This way we can keep track of how many times an individual has been deported, as well as to see if they are wanted for other crimes."

Bob points out that while carrying out the law is a duty he takes pride in, he's often touched by those aliens who've sacrificed a great deal in order to come to the United States. "I've heard stories from people about how they've sold all their belongings to finance the trip, or how they were robbed by bandits," he says sympathetically. "But through all of this, you still have to do your job, which is enforcing U.S. immigration law." On the other hand, Bob says that he gets immense job satisfaction after helping to intercept a large narcotics shipment or putting a dent into an organized alien smuggling ring's operation.

HAVE I GOT WHAT IT TAKES TO BE A BPO?

Being a border patrol officer requires a unique blend of qualities that include toughness, compassion, the ability to work under stress, and quick decision-making skills. An officer must be able to analyze a situation on the spot and have the ability to calmly defuse a volatile moment. "Good officers have even tempers and use their imagination to deal with constantly changing work conditions, personalities, and even changes in the law," says Bob.

An officer also needs to be compassionate. Many people who attempt to enter the United States illegally have undergone extreme risk and hardship, and border patrol officers just as frequently encounter emotionally moving situations as hostile, violent ones. Officers must be able to work at enforcing what, at times, may seem a futile and frustrating task. Bob notes, "The hardest part of the job comes after you've arrested a person, and he begins telling you what he's gone through to come to the United States. After you hear their stories, you can understand why they're trying to sneak in, and you can imagine yourself doing the same if the situation was reversed."

To be a successful border patrol officer, you should:

Be tough, yet compassionate, when apprehending illegal aliens

Be able to work under stress and in physically demanding environments

Have a strong sense of direction and experience with the geography of wilderness areas

Be well organized and motivated

Be able to communicate effectively in writing, since there is a certain amount of paperwork and reports involved

Be able to speak fluent Spanish

Border patrol officers also need to have a strong sense of direction and experience with the geography of wilderness areas. Because they work long shifts in sometimes harsh terrain, it's absolutely vital that a border patrol officer have physical stamina and strength.

Because they often work with little supervision, border patrol officers should be able to plan and organize their own work schedule. They should be able to communicate effectively in writing, since there is a certain amount of paperwork and reports involved.

HOW DO I BECOME A BORDER PATROL OFFICER?

EDUCATION

High School

A high school diploma, or its equivalent, is the minimum requirement to apply for a position with the Border Patrol. A bachelor's degree, however, is preferred. Of the classes that Bob took in high school, the one that he says helps the most in his job was Junior ROTC. "It began laying the foundation of discipline and the mindset that I could do anything I set my mind to." He also suggests finding a volunteer program—such as Boy Scout Explorers—through the local police station or fire station for hands-on experience in law enforcement.

He recommends that high school students who are interested in working for the Border Patrol take courses in Spanish to set a good foundation to build on. "The most common reason for people failing their probationary year with the patrol is their Spanish skills," he says. A solid understanding of the basic rules of English also help, since good communication skills are crucial to pass the written entrance exam, as well as once you're in the training academy and on the job.

Postsecondary Training

For the high school graduate with a strong interest in becoming a border patrol officer, a bachelor's degree in criminal justice, criminology, or law enforcement is recommended. These areas of study will introduce you to immigration law. And again, studying Spanish in college could give candidates a solid head start, since the amount of language taught during the training academy is equivalent to two years of college-level Spanish.

Bob has some bits of specific advice: "If college funds are not a problem, then I'd suggest going to college and earning a law-related degree, with a minor in Spanish. Another route is through the military, which provides the training, maturity, and discipline. Plus it can be a great way to save money for college."

In the Chula Vista sector, there is an internship available to students majoring in criminal science or criminal justice. Similar internships are also available elsewhere.

On-the-Job Training

Everyone hired as a border patrol officer has to complete an eighteen-week training academy in either Glynco, Georgia, or Charleston, South Carolina. At the academy, trainees receive intensive instruction in Spanish, immigration and nationality law, firearms, judo and physical training, arrest methods, methods of tracking and surveillance, self-defense, court procedures, as well as report writing, fingerprinting, care and use of firearms, and pursuit driving.

Bob notes that border patrol officers have to become extremely knowledgeable in immigration law and that some background courses in college can be useful. "The average trainee spends five hours each day just studying law," he says.

After graduation, the trainee reports to his or her duty station and attends a post-academy class once a week. This training focuses on law instruction and Spanish language. During the first ten months of employment, the trainee's progress is graded two times. He or she must pass a Spanish and law exam after six months on the job, and the final test is given after ten months.

LABOR UNIONS

Bob is a member of the National Border Patrol Council, a small union specifically for border patrol officers. The union is recommended but not required. It protects officers against unfair labor practices and disciplinary actions, and also works to improve working conditions and salaries.

WHO WILL HIRE ME?

There's no question of who your employer will be if you enter this field. All border patrol officers are employees of the Department of Justice's Immigration and Naturalization Service (INS). The INS accepts applications during a certain period of time known as an "open period." You can write or call the INS to find out when this period is and to get an application (see information under "Look to the Pros"). Basic qualifications for consideration by the Border Patrol

WHO WILL HIRE ME?, CONTINUED

include the following: you must also be a U.S. citizen, between the ages of twenty-one and thirty-seven, have a valid driver's license, and not have a criminal record.

The first step in applying for the Border Patrol involves taking a written U.S. Office of Personnel Management entrance exam. Those who earn high test scores will go on a list of eligible applicants who are granted interviews. If the interview goes well, candidates take a medical exam which includes a urine drug test and will also undergo background checks. The entire process described above can take a matter of months. However, there is also an expedited hiring process for those willing to travel to certain testing and interview sites at their own expense. Ask about it when you contact the INS.

If you are selected and hired (on a probationary basis), the next stop is the eighteen-week training academy described earlier in this chapter. After the training, new border patrol officers are initially assigned to southern border stations. These assignments are made according to manpower needs at each sector, and new officers are not given a choice of their first duty station. Later in your career, you can request particular stations, although transfers to the northern stations along the U.S.-Canada border are rare and hard to get.

WHERE CAN I GO FROM HERE?

Bob says he's happy to have earned promotions during his eleven years with the Border Patrol to be in his current position as Senior Patrol Agent at Chula Vista. He has also served as a temporary supervisor at times, and sees himself eventually transferring to a station in Arizona or New Mexico as a supervisor.

Advancement Possibilities

Senior patrol officers *are experienced officers who train and oversee new border patrol officers.*

Border patrol supervisors *oversee the staff of a border patrol station.*

Special agents *conduct investigations on violations of INS laws.*

Immigrations inspectors *arrest violators of INS laws at entry points to the United States.*

Deportation officers *are responsible for deporting aliens who have violated immigration laws.*

Overall, there are good prospects for advancement as a border patrol officer. Officers are hired at the GS-5 or GS-7 level, depending on the level of their education. Generally, entry at the GS-7 level is for those in the Outstanding Scholar's Program, which requires a grade-point average of 3.5 or higher during specified periods of an applicant's college career. After completing a six-month probationary period, all other new officers are promoted to GS-7; a year later, they are advanced to the GS-9 journeyman level. From that point on, promotions are granted on a competitive basis. The next step up is Senior Patrol Officer (GS-11) and then Supervisory Border Patrol Officer (GS-12). Border patrol officers can also work in other areas with the Immigration and Naturalization Service, becoming an immigration inspector, special agent, or deportation officer, for instance.

There are also opportunities with other law enforcement agencies. "Because of the length and intensity of our training academy," says Bob, "officers have no problem transferring to other agencies." These might include the U.S. Marshals, the Federal Bureau of Investigation, the Drug Enforcement Agency (DEA), and U.S. Customs. "The DEA hires quite a few of our agents because of their fluency in the Spanish language," Bob says.

WHAT ARE SOME RELATED JOBS?

The U.S. Department of Labor classifies border patrol officers under the headings Occupations in Law and Order, Public Service, Investigating, and Immigration and Customs Work. Included in these categories are people who investigate illegal activities and arrest those who violate laws.

Within the Immigration and Naturalization Service, there are several jobs closely related to border patrol officer, such as *special agents,* who conduct investigations on violations of INS laws; *immigration inspectors,* who arrest violators of INS laws at entry points to the United States; and *deportation officers,* who are responsible for deporting aliens who have violated immigration laws. There are also other service jobs within the INS that involve administering interviews or examinations of people who wish to become naturalized citizens.

Related Jobs

Bailiffs

Deputy sheriffs

Detectives

Fingerprint classifiers

Fish and game wardens

Intelligence specialists

Internal affairs investigators

Narcotics investigators

Park rangers

Police officers

Private investigators

State highway patrol officers

Undercover operators

WHAT ARE THE SALARY RANGES?

Starting salaries for a new agent are $34,000 in the first year. A journeyman agent (GS-9) earns about $43,000, a senior agent (GS-11) can expect about $56,000, and a supervisor of a station (GS-12) earns around $67,000. Because these are federal jobs, the salaries are generally higher than comparable law enforcement jobs with city,

What Are the Salary Ranges ?, continued

county, or state agencies would be. Other benefits include sick time and vacation time (the accrual rate for vacation time increases with years of service). Any injuries incurred on the job are covered by a government plan. There is also a choice of health plans for border patrol officers, depending upon where they are stationed. Officers can save for retirement under the Federal Employee Retirement System (FERS) and may also enroll in the Thrift Savings Plan.

What Is the Job Outlook?

"I've seen the size of my station and the Border Patrol as a whole grow at a fast pace in the eleven years I've been an officer," says Bob. In fact, the size of his station has more than quadrupled. In 1986, there were about one hundred officers assigned to the Chula Vista station; now, there are nearly five hundred.

This growth can largely be attributed to the United States government's expanded effort to curb the increase in smuggling and illegal immigration along the Mexico border. In 1996, the Immigration and Naturalization Service was one of the few federal agencies to receive approval from Congress for a budget increase. As a result, 1,000 new border patrol officers were hired—a 20 percent increase in the size of the force. More job openings are expected in the future as well, thanks to better public awareness about illegal immigration and ongoing government-backed efforts to crack down on drug smuggling.

It is important to note, however, that these are regarded as desirable federal jobs, and because of rigorous hiring standards, the competition is always stiff. After the initial probationary period, the job security for a border patrol officer is good. There is very low turnover in the field, especially compared to other law enforcement positions.

Corrections Officer

SUMMARY

DEFINITION
Corrections officers *guard people who have been arrested and are awaiting trial or who have been tried, convicted, and sentenced to serve time in a penal institution.*

ALTERNATIVE JOB TITLES
Correctional officer
Detentions officer
Jailer

SALARY RANGE
$19,100 to $28,300 to $55,000

EDUCATIONAL REQUIREMENTS
High school diploma

CERTIFICATION OR LICENSING
Not mandatory, but useful for certain job functions

EMPLOYMENT OUTLOOK
Faster than the average

HIGH SCHOOL SUBJECTS
Government
Physical education
Psychology
Sociology

PERSONAL INTERESTS
Exercise/Personal fitness
Helping people: emotionally
Law
Sports
Student government

An hour ago, corrections officer David Pilgrim was chatting with a convicted murderer in the Oklahoma State Penitentiary about today's lineup of college football games. The man admitted a soft spot for his home state's team and asked if David would find out what the final score was.

That conversation was a pleasant change from the beginning of David's shift, when a fight broke out between two inmates in the showers. One inmate had cleverly crafted a knife out of his plastic light shade and took it into the shower with him. Fortunately, the man had dropped the knife the instant David stepped in.

Now David has rolled up the shirt sleeves of his dark blue uniform and is wrist-deep in an enormous vat of green beans. "I take myself pretty seriously at times like this," he jokes with another officer, jabbing a thermometer into the beans to test that they're heated to the correct temperature. He dishes up a plate and hands the tray to one of the inmate workers, who will deliver it to the others. Once meals are served to all ninety-eight inmates on his floor, David will take a few minutes to eat his own dinner that he packed from home. Then it'll be time for him to walk the hallways for another routine head count.

WHAT DOES A CORRECTIONS OFFICER DO?

Corrections officers are hired by federal, state, and local prisons and jails to maintain order according to the institution's policies, regulations, and procedures. They are concerned with the safekeeping of people who have been arrested and are awaiting trial or who have been tried, found guilty, and are serving time in a correctional institution.

Corrections officers keep watch over inmates around the clock—while they're eating, sleeping, exercising, bathing, and working. In order to prevent disturbances, corrections officers carefully observe the conduct and behavior of inmates. They watch for forbidden activities, as well as for poor adjustment to prison life. They try to settle disputes before violence can erupt. They may search the inmates or their living quarters for weapons or drugs and inspect locks, bars on windows and doors, and gates for any sign of tampering. They conduct regular head counts to make sure all inmates are accounted for. Some corrections officers are stationed on towers and at gates to prevent escapes. In the case of a major disturbance, a corrections officer may have to use a weapon or force. After such a violation or disturbance, corrections officers are responsible for filing detailed reports. Corrections officers cannot show favoritism and must report any inmate who breaks the rules.

Corrections officers assign work projects to the inmates, supervise them while they carry out their work, and teach them about unfamiliar tasks. Officers try to ensure inmates' health and safety by checking the cells for unsanitary conditions and fire hazards. They are in charge of screening visitors at the entrance and inspecting mail for prohibited items. Officers are also responsible for escorting inmates from one area of the prison to another and helping them get medical assistance. Certain officers are charged with transporting inmates between courthouses, prisons, mental institutions, or other destinations.

Some officers specialize in guarding juvenile offenders who are being held at a police station or detention house pending a hearing. These officers often investigate the background of first offenders to check for a criminal history and to make a recommendation to the court. Lost or runaway children are also placed in the custody of these officers until their parents or guardians can be contacted. In small commu-

Lingo to Learn

Contraband: *Any forbidden item that is in a prisoner's possession.*

House: *An inmate will refer to his cell as his "house."*

Run: *A hallway lined with inmates' cells.*

Shake-down: *Corrections officers conduct a thorough search of an inmate's cell, looking for contraband.*

Yard-out: *This means that it's time for the inmates to go to the yard for exercise. Correctional officers also say "chow-out" when it's time for the inmates to eat and "shower-out" when it's time for showers.*

Just Who Lands in a Federal Prison?

If you go to work in the federal prisons, do you wonder about what kind of criminals you'll be dealing with? It might surprise you to learn that drug offenses far and away bring the most people to federal prison. A whopping 60.2 percent of inmates in federal prisons committed crimes involving drugs. Robbers account for 9.6 percent of the inmates; firearms, explosives, arson 9.0 percent; property offenses 5.9 percent; extortion, fraud, bribery 5.6 percent; immigration 3.4 percent; violent offenses 2.6 percent; other 1.5 percent; continuing criminal enterprise 0.8 percent; white collar 0.7 percent; courts or corrections 0.6 percent; and national security 0.1 percent.

nities, corrections officers may also serve as deputy sheriffs or police officers.

The person in charge of supervising other corrections officers is often called the *head corrections officer.* This person assigns duties, directs the activities of groups of inmates, arranges for the release and transfer of inmates, and maintains overall security measures.

While psychologists and social workers work at the prison to counsel inmates, a secondary aspect of a corrections officer's job is to provide informal counseling. Officers may talk with inmates in order to help them adjust to prison life, prepare for return to civilian life, and avoid committing crimes in the future. On a more immediate level, they can help inmates arrange a visit to the library, get in touch with their families, suggest how to look for a job after being released from prison, or discuss personal problems. Corrections officers who have college degrees in psychology or criminology often take on these more rehabilitative responsibilities.

Corrections officers keep a daily record of their activities and make regular reports to their supervisors. These reports concern the behavior of the inmates, the quality and quantity of work they do, as well as any disturbances, rule violations, and unusual occurrences. Because prison security has to be maintained at all times, corrections officers sometimes are expected to work nights, weekends, and holidays. Generally, a work week consists of five eight-hour days. Work takes place both indoors and outdoors, depending on the officer's assigned duties on a given day. Conditions range from a well-lit, well-ventilated area to a hot, noisy, and overcrowded one.

WHAT IS IT LIKE TO BE A CORRECTIONS OFFICER?

David Pilgrim is a corrections officer with the rank of sergeant at the Oklahoma State Penitentiary, a maximum-security facility housing fourteen hundred inmates. He's thirty-three years old and has worked at the prison for three years. During this time, he has been promoted twice and was recently named Outstanding Correctional Officer at his facility.

Much of his work is routine, but he has to be prepared for violence to erupt at any time. As a matter of fact, that's one of the things David will tell you right off the bat that he likes about his job. "It's the unpredictability," he says. "I like the notion that anything could happen when I go for a shift." His current shift runs from 2 PM to 10 PM, with Wednesdays and Thursdays off. He begins the workday by attending a briefing fifteen minutes before his shift begins. Here, he and the other corrections officers going on duty find out everything that's happened and learn which unit they'll be working that day, if they don't have a permanent assignment.

//Doing the count and recording it in the log is routine, and following a routine is important here."

Once he gets to the unit, the first order of business is to take a count of inmates, which he'll repeat at two-hour intervals. "Doing the count and recording it in the log is routine, and following a routine is important here." Absolutely everything that happens during a shift, from the mundane to the extraordinary, must be documented in this log. His shift is likely to include escorting small groups of inmates to the shower or out to the yard for exercise. At mealtime, he and the other officers are responsible for dishing up the meals, which are delivered to inmates' cells by other inmates granted "worker" status.

Beyond those routine tasks, David says he deals with "whatever breaks out." Attempted suicides, knife fights, and feigned illness are all standard fare. "Last night," he says, "a couple of them taped the doors up in their cell and jammed books in the locks because they were conducting a gang initiation." But he emphasizes that a good deal of his work is not so tense. "The inmates like to hear what's going on in the outside world. They're always real interested in what I brought for lunch, because the food in here, is . . . well . . . ," he says.

Talking to inmates and to fellow officers is one of the things David most enjoys. "Some folks like being assigned to the towers or to the control room, but that's torture to me. You're just sitting there alone waiting for your shift to go by." As a sergeant, David particularly likes being able to help and coach the new officers assigned to him for on-the-job training. "I'm very security-minded and I try to pass that on to the cadets," he says.

Unlike most of his peers at the prison, David has a bachelor's degree. He majored in wildlife conservation, with the expectation that he'd become a game warden. But he discovered that it was difficult to break into that field. At the prison, he's actually made greater use of his minor in occupational safety and health. This background has been extremely useful, he notes, because sanitation is a major concern among corrections officers. "You treat everyone as though they have HIV, because so many of the inmates do. We wear rubber gloves whenever we're in direct contact."

The Oklahoma State Penitentiary is under twenty-three-hour lockdown, which means that corrections officers must escort inmates everywhere that they go. "Sometimes it seems like a big daycare," jokes David. Officers there don't carry weapons on them and instead keep anything that could be used against them—like restraints, handcuffs, and weapons—in the control rooms. The officers rely on radios and an intercom system to communicate with one another when a need arises.

HAVE I GOT WHAT IT TAKES TO BE A CORRECTIONS OFFICER?

There's no denying that handling the inherent stress of this line of work takes a unique person. In a maximum-security facility, the environment is often noisy, crowded, poorly ventilated, and even dangerous. Corrections officers need the physical and emotional strength to handle the stress involved in working with criminals, some of whom may be violent. A corrections officer has to stay alert and aware of prisoners' actions and attitudes. This constant vigilance can be harder on some people. Work in a minimum-security prison is usually more comfortable, cleaner, and less stressful.

Officers need to use persuasion rather than brute force to get inmates to follow the rules. Certain inmates take a disproportionate amount of time and attention because they're either violent, mentally ill, or victims of abuse by other inmates. Officers have to carry out routine duties while being alert for the unpredictable outbursts. Sound judgment and the ability to think and act quickly are important

To be a successful corrections officer, you should:

Not be easily intimidated or influenced by the inmates

Have physical and emotional strength to handle sometimes violent or abusive prisoners

Be able to use persuasion rather than brute force to get inmates to follow the rules

Be able to stay alert and aware of prisoners' actions and attitudes

Have sound judgment and the ability to think and act quickly

Be able to communicate clearly both verbally and in writing

qualities for corrections officers. "We have quite a few new cadets who freeze up when the first fight breaks out among inmates," David says. "It takes a while before I feel comfortable putting my life in the hands of someone who hasn't been tested." With experience and training, corrections officers are usually able to handle volatile situations without resorting to physical force.

The ability to communicate clearly verbally and in writing is extremely important. "You've got to be able to get across to all walks of life," David says. Corrections officers have to write a number of reports, documenting routine procedures as well as any violations by the inmates. David's eight-hour shift can easily extend to ten hours because of the reports that must be written.

An effective corrections officer is not easily intimidated or influenced by the inmates. There's a misconception, however, that corrections officers need to be tough guys. While it's true that a person needs some physical strength to perform the job, machismo only gets in the way. "You get types who think that with a badge on they can do and say anything," David says. "That attitude will only get you injured. If I'm in a unit without air conditioning on a hot day, the inmates get awfully irritated and may verbally abuse me when I walk by. There's no sense in doing anything but to keep on walking."

HOW DO I BECOME A CORRECTIONS OFFICER?

EDUCATION

High School
Entry requirements vary widely from state to state. A high school diploma, or its equivalent, is the minimum requirement for employment at most correctional institutions. While most high school classes are not directly relevant to corrections, health classes may offer an introduction to issues that will be covered thoroughly during formal training as a corrections officer, such as sanitation, universal precautions, and first aid.

English classes are recommended as well for anyone interested in a career as a corrections officer. At most prisons, jails, and penitentiaries, reports are required to be well-written, with attention paid to sentence structure and spelling. David commented that officers who write sloppy reports are often the last to be promoted. Spanish would also be useful for future corrections officers who plan on working in a region of the country with a large Spanish-speaking population.

Postsecondary Training

Some correctional institutions require that corrections officers possess a college degree. In certain states, officers need two years of college with an emphasis on criminal justice or behavioral science, or three years as a correctional, military police, or licensed peace officer. Generally, states that require more education offer higher entry-level salaries and have shorter-duration training academies. At federal institutions, applicants must have at least two years of college or two years of work or military experience.

The most relevant areas of study in college include psychology, criminal justice, police science, and criminology. Some correctional facilities offer internships to students who are earning their degrees in these areas.

CERTIFICATION AND TRAINING

The American Correctional Association and the American Jail Association provide guidelines for prison training programs. These programs generally introduce new corrections officers to the policies of their particular institution and prepare them for handling work situations. The training lasts several weeks and includes crisis intervention, contraband control, counseling, self-defense, and use of firearms.

Training ranges from special academies to informal, on-the-job training. The Federal Bureau of Prisons operates its training center in Glynco, Georgia, where new hires take part in a three-week training program. In Oklahoma, new hires work for a month to "try the career on" before going to the six-week training academy. After the training academy, a new officer will usually spend two to six months under the supervision of an experienced officer.

While there are numerous certifications available to corrections officers, these are optional in most states. Common certifications include self-defense, weapons use, urine analysis, shield and gun, shotgun/handgun, CPR, and cell extraction. Many officers also take advantage of additional training that is offered at their facility, such as suicide prevention, AIDS awareness, use of four-point restraints, and emergency preparedness. At most prisons, there is annual mandatory in-service training that focuses on policies and procedures.

LABOR UNIONS

Union membership is not required, but many correctional officers find it advantageous to join. Officers who work for state-run facilities can join the union for all state employees. In return for weekly or monthly dues, members receive services intended to improve their working conditions. David says that

HOW DO I BECOME A . . . ?, CONTINUED

he joined his union recently but has not become very involved yet. Currently, his union is focusing on rising concerns among Oklahoma correctional officers about the extreme shortage of staff, overtime pay, and safety issues.

WHO WILL HIRE ME?

There are facilities in virtually every part of the country that need corrections officers. You could work in a prison or jail that houses men, women, juveniles, or a combination. Roughly 60 percent of officers work in state-run facilities. Many others are employed at city and county jails, while the smallest percentage works for the federal government. A number of officers are hired by privately run correctional facilities. Depending where you live, you may also have the choice of maximum-, medium-, and minimum-security facilities.

To apply for a job, simply contact your state's department of corrections or the Federal Bureau of Prisons and request information about entrance requirements, training, and job opportunities. In addition, there are numerous journals that include a list of job openings. For example, three of the professional organizations listed at the end of this book—the American Correctional Association, the International Association of Correctional Officers, and the Federal Bureau of Prisons—have both publications and Web sites with job listings. Other publications that post job openings are *Corrections Compendium* and *Inside Corrections.*

Most correctional institutions require candidates to be at least eighteen years old (sometimes twenty-one years old), have a high school diploma, and be a U.S. citizen with no criminal record. There are also health and physical strength requirements, and many states have minimum height, vision, and hearing standards. Other common requirements are a driver's license and a job record that shows you've been dependable.

WHERE CAN I GO FROM HERE?

David feels that his facility offers good opportunities for advancement. He began as a cadet, was promoted to corrections officer I, then corporal, and now sergeant. He envisions himself moving into counseling or case management, and eventually unit management. He says that his college degree has probably helped differentiate him when he has applied for promotions, but that an excellent performance record is important, too.

Advancement possibilities

Head corrections officers supervise other corrections officers. They assign duties, direct the activities of inmates, arrange the release and transfer of inmates, and maintain overall security measures.

Wardens, sometimes known as prison directors, oversee all correctional staff. They are ultimately responsible for the safety of the prisoner population, as well as the security of the prison and its employees.

Probation and parole officers monitor and counsel offenders, process their release from prison, and evaluate their progress in becoming productive members of society.

Many officers take college courses in law enforcement or criminal justice to increase their chances of promotion. In some states, officers must serve two years in each position before they can be considered for a promotion. Training officer Wayne Ternes at the Montana State Prison says his facility is seeing more college graduates applying for the position of corrections officer. "They see that it's not just a job to fill the time until something better comes along. It's an excellent career path." Wayne himself began as a corrections officer, and then worked in food service, all the while with his eye on training.

With additional education and training, experienced officers can also be promoted to supervisory or administrative positions such as *head corrections officer, assistant warden,* or *prison director.* Officers who want to continue to work directly with offenders can move into various other positions. For example, *probation and parole officers* monitor and counsel offenders, process their release from prison, and evaluate their progress in becoming productive members of society. *Recreation leaders* organize and instruct offenders in sports, games, and arts and crafts.

WHAT ARE SOME RELATED JOBS?

The U.S. Department of Labor classifies corrections officers with workers in detention occupations and in protective service occupations. Included in these categories are people who guard prisoner at institutions other than prisons and jails, such as mental institutions or courthouses; people who maintain law and order during courtroom proceedings, such as *bailiffs*; or people who prevent crime, such as *security guards* and *police officers.* Some of these related jobs include armored car guards, security guards, bodyguards, bailiffs, parole officers, patrol conductors, probation officers, police officers, immigration guards, firefighters, and fish and game wardens.

Related Jobs

Armored car guards

Bailiffs

Bodyguards

Fire fighters

Fish and game wardens

Immigration guards

Parole officers

Patrol conductors

Police officers

Probation officers

Security guards

WHAT ARE THE SALARY RANGES?

According to a 1996 survey in *Corrections Compendium,* the national journal for corrections officers, salaries of corrections officers vary dramatically from institution to institution. Entry-level salaries at state-run facilities, for instance, range from $12,930 to $31,805. Salaries of experienced corrections officers at state facilities range from $17,300 to $41,730.

At the federal level, starting salaries were about $19,000 in 1994. Federal officers with several years of experience earned about $30,000, and supervisory officers at the federal level averaged around $55,000.

Most corrections officers participate in medical and dental insurance plans offered by their facility, and can get disability and life insurance at group rates. They also receive vacation and sick leave, as well as retirement benefits. Many correctional facilities, such as the Oklahoma Department of Corrections, offer full retirement benefits for corrections officers after twenty years of service.

WHAT IS THE JOB OUTLOOK?

Corrections officers can count on steady employment and good job security. Prison security has to be maintained at all times, making corrections officers unlikely candidates for layoffs, even when there are budget cuts. These jobs are rarely affected by changes in the economy or government spending. Due to a high turnover rate, a budget can usually be trimmed by simply not replacing the officers who leave voluntarily.

There are other factors pointing to the strong job outlook for corrections officers. The prison population has more than doubled in the past ten years, and new prisons are being built to house these inmates. This growth is expected to continue, with the trend in the United States being toward mandatory sentencing guidelines, longer sentences, and reduced parole. All of this translates into a strong need for more corrections officers. It is estimated that another 103,000 jobs will be created by the year 2006, an increase in employment of 61 percent. While entry-level jobs are plentiful, competition will continue to be stiff for the higher-paying supervisory jobs.

Certain technological developments—such as closed-circuit television, computer tracking systems, and automatic gates—do allow a single corrections officer to monitor a number of prisoners from a centralized location, but the impact of these technologies on overall staffing needs is minimal.

Crime Analyst

SUMMARY

DEFINITION
Crime analysts *analyze patterns in criminal behavior in order to catch criminals, predict patterns and motives of criminals, and improve the responsiveness of law enforcement agencies.*

ALTERNATIVE JOB TITLES
None

SALARY RANGE
$24,000 to $37,000 to $60,000

EDUCATIONAL REQUIREMENTS
College degree highly recommended

CERTIFICATION OR LICENSING
Not required. Currently, only California offers a state-sponsored certification program.

EMPLOYMENT OUTLOOK
Faster than the average

HIGH SCHOOL SUBJECTS
Computer science
English (writing/literature)
Psychology
Sociology

PERSONAL INTERESTS
Computers
Figuring out how things work
Helping people: protection
Reading/Books

A police radio drones in the background while Michelle Rankin quickly reads through crime reports from all of the area police stations. She is just beginning to type up a daily bulletin encapsulating the "hot" crime investigations when she hears something that catches her attention over the radio.

She shifts her chair to turn up the volume. Police officers from her department are investigating a report of a sexual assault, and they've got the suspect's name but little else to go on. She turns back to her computer, closes out one database, and pulls up the local system. A search for the man's name doesn't turn up anything that would indicate he's had prior contact with local police.

Next, Michelle runs his name through the state system. Here, his name is on file as a known sex offender. A new law in the state of California allows the photos and addresses of all sex registrants to be issued quarterly on CD-ROM to police departments. Michelle inserts the disk into her computer drive, pulls up the man's mug shot, and prints out copies. In less than half an hour after the radio report, officers on the beat have photos of the suspect to work from. When they spot him on the street, they're able to move in and make an arrest.

Meanwhile, Michelle has already finished writing her daily bulletin and has turned her attention to three retail store robberies that she's noticed have striking similarities. Between bites of a sandwich for dinner, she's busy pulling files to analyze details of each case.

WHAT DOES A CRIME ANALYST DO?

Crime analysts try to uncover and piece together information about crime patterns, crime trends, and criminal suspects. It's a job that varies wildly from day to day and from one law enforcement agency to the next. At its core is a systematic process that involves collecting, categorizing, analyzing, and sharing information in order to help the agency that a crime analyst works for to better deploy officers on the street, work through difficult investigations, and increase arrests of criminals.

The basic work of a crime analyst involves collecting crime data from a range of sources, including police reports, statewide computer databases, crime newsletters, word-of-mouth tips, and interviews with suspects. To be of use, this information is then analyzed for patterns. Crime analysts are constantly vigilant for details that are similar or familiar. In addition to specific crime data, a crime analyst might study general factors such as population density, the demographic makeup of the population, commuting patterns, economic conditions (average income, poverty level, job availability), effectiveness of law enforcement agencies, citizens' attitudes toward crime, and crime reporting practices.

The responsibilities of a crime analyst are often dependent upon the needs of their police department or law enforcement agency. One morning's tasks might include writing a profile on a particular demographic group's criminal patterns. On another day, an analyst could meet with the police chief to discuss an unusual string of local car thefts. Less frequently, the work includes going on "ride-alongs" with street cops, visiting a crime scene, or meeting with crime analysts from surrounding jurisdictions to exchange information about criminals who are plaguing the region. Occasionally, a crime analyst is pulled off of everyday responsibilities in order to work exclusively on a task force, usually focusing on a rash of violent crimes. As an ongoing responsibility, a crime analyst might be charged with

Lingo to Learn

Cluster analysis: *A computerized analysis of where specific crimes are happening. This tool identifies crime "hot spots."*

Crime pattern: *The occurrence of similar crimes in a defined geographic area.*

Crime series: *A crime pattern where there is reason to believe that the same suspect is responsible for the crimes.*

GIS: *Geographic information systems—a mapping software commonly used in crime analysis.*

Intelligence analysis: *The study of relationships between people, organizations, and events. This applies to organized crime, conspiratorial acts like money laundering, crime rings like auto theft or child pornography, or other crimes of corruption.*

Investigative analysis: *The study of why a person is committing crimes of a serial nature.*

M.O.: *Mode of operation—the standard way, or pattern, in which a particular criminal commits a crime.*

Crime Confusion

In a field like crime analysis, there's sometimes confusion about who does what. The quickest way to tick off a crime analyst is to say something about their lab coats. (Hint: They don't wear lab coats, nor do they spend their days in laboratories.) So, here are a few professions with titles that might sound a lot like crime analyst, but are actually different careers.

Crime scene evidence technicians *go to the scene of the crime in order to collect and photograph relevant evidence, such as fingerprints, hairs, bullets, etc.*

Criminalists *scientifically analyze, compare, and evaluate physical evidence in the laboratory.*

Criminologists *study and research crime from a sociological perspective. They usually work in a university setting, rather than for a law enforcement agency.*

Forensic psychologists *make psychological evaluations based on criminal evidence or behavior.*

tracking and monitoring "known offenders" (sex offenders, career criminals, repeat juvenile offenders, and parolees).

New computer technology has had a profound impact on the profession of crime analysis, helping it grow by leaps and bounds. In its earliest days, crime analysis simply meant gathering straight statistics on crime. Now these same statistics—coupled with specialized software—allow crime analysts to actually predict and prevent criminal activity.

The use of this analysis falls into three broad categories: tactical, strategic, and administrative. Tactical crime analysis aims at giving police officers and detectives prompt, in-the-field information that could lead to an arrest. These are the "hot" items that land on a crime analyst's desk, usually pertaining to specific crimes and offenders. For example, a criminal's mode of operation (M.O.) can be studied in order to predict who the likely next targets or victims will be. The police can then set up stakeouts or saturate the area with patrol cars. Tactical analysis is also used to do crime-suspect correlation, which involves identifying suspects for certain crimes based on their criminal histories.

Strategic analysis deals with finding solutions to long-range problems and crime trends. For instance, a crime analyst could create a crime trend forecast, based on current and past criminal activity, using computer software. An analyst might also perform a "manpower deployment" study to see if the police department is making best use of its personnel. Another aspect of strategic analysis involves collating and disseminating demographic data on victims and geographic areas experiencing high crime rates so that the police are able to beef up crime prevention efforts.

Lastly, administrative analysis helps to provide policy-making information to a police department's administration. This might include a statistical study on the activity levels of police officers that would support a request for hiring more officers. Administrative work could also include creating graphs and charts that are used in management presentations or writing a speech on local crime prevention to give to the city council.

WHAT IS IT LIKE TO BE A CRIME ANALYST?

Michelle Rankin is an articulate and engaging twenty-seven-year-old who in five years has worked her way from being a volunteer in a southern California police department's crime analysis unit to head of a new unit in Santa Clara, a town of 98,000 in northern California. The first thing that strikes you about Michelle is simply how many things she can do at once. While carrying on a phone conversation, she's also flipping through newsletters on her desk and jotting down files she wants to pull. She says there's never an empty "in" box on her desk and acknowledges that work can become hectic when several important requests land on her desk. "Staying flexible, re-prioritizing, and multi-tasking—that's just part of the job," she says. "Some days you can be proactive, and other days, you just work through the requests."

On a typical day (which she insists doesn't really exist), Michelle will write a daily bulletin after reading through numerous reports and pulling out serious items. She'll talk with detectives to see if they need some piece of information that she can help get the word out about. She sees herself as a question-and-answer unit for people in the department. "An officer might tell me about an unusual burglary, and I can search for other burglaries that have similarities." At other times, she gets wind of something herself and initiates a search. "An officer on one side of town doesn't usually know what's occurred on the other side. Since I read crime reports from all over, I can bridge the gap and piece together information that links back to the same suspect." Powerful software such as databases, spreadsheets, and geographic mapping systems help her perform certain aspects of her job. With a mapping system, for instance, Michelle can create a map that shows where Honda Accords have been stolen or where burglaries of only jewelry have occurred. This information can in turn be used to narrow down the list of suspects.

Sometimes a crime analyst puts the pieces together only *after* a suspect has been arrested, but prior to a court date. After a series of daytime residential burglaries, for example, a crime analyst might create a map showing that each of the burglaries was within a one-mile radius of a certain juvenile offender's house. Compiled with information about the juvenile's school attendance, this map could be used as evidence in court.

In order to have contact with officers working graveyard and swing shifts—as well as day shifts—Michelle works different shifts every two weeks. Building these in-house connections is the bedrock of doing good crime analysis. Another crime analyst, Judy Kimminau, who works in a comparably sized police department in Fort Collins, Colorado, says, "Without good relationships with the officers, you simply don't get good information." Crime analysts in newly established units often have to work at winning over police officers. "Sometimes I'll come up with a good lead, but the officer on the beat doesn't take it up," Michelle says. "You need to have tough skin and focus on working with those who want to work with you."

If there are serious frustrations on the job for Michelle, they have to do with the department's antiquated computer records system. "It wasn't set up to perform some of the more complex inquiries. Instead, I'd have to pull hundreds of files by hand to get one little piece of data." Fortunately, this system is on the way out the door. The department is selecting a new information management system, and Michelle has been a part of that decision-making process.

Michelle also serves as vice president of the California Crime Analysts Association's Bay Area chapter, which meets regularly. Since there's often only one crime analyst working in each agency, they rely on a wider network to stay abreast of new concepts in the field, share their observations, and to check out new software. And in fact, as a relatively new and small field, many crime analysts nationwide are familiar with one another, particularly those who are active in the International Association of Crime Analysts (IACA).

HAVE I GOT WHAT IT TAKES TO BE A CRIME ANALYST?

A crime analyst needs to be inquisitive, logical, and have a good memory for what they hear and read. "You get a feel for it after a while," Michelle says. She tells of reading a teletype recently that described a suspect in a bank robbery. "Something about the description of his nose and hairline rung a bell," she says. By combing through some old teletypes, she found a similar description and called the agency that had arrested the man before. In doing so, she was able to uncover the man's name and obtain a photo of him that matched a surveillance photo from the bank.

A willingness to dig in and do this sort of research is important, since much of the work involves piecing together disparate bits of information. Ask Steven Gottlieb, MPA, an internationally recognized crime analysis trainer, consultant, and executive director of the Alpha Group Center for Crime and Intelligence Analysis, just who will make a good crime analyst and he laughs, "Somebody

To be a successful crime analyst, you should:

Be inquisitive, logical, and have a photographic memory for details

Have excellent research skills

Have a strong stomach for sometimes graphic or disturbing crime information

Be able to work as a member of a law enforcement team and not always be in the limelight who does crossword puzzles in ink." He explains that crime analysts love the process of working with bits of data that in and of themselves mean nothing. "It's only when you put them together that a clear picture emerges," he says.

Even though crime analysts aren't out on the streets, they're immersed in the law enforcement milieu and come into contact with information that's potentially disturbing. "If a person becomes especially upset after reading reports on a murder or a child's molestation in the newspaper or after seeing a crime scene photo on television," notes Judy Kimminau, "they're probably not cut out for this line of work."

> **//If a person becomes especially upset after reading reports on a murder . . . or after seeing a crime scene photo on television, they're probably not cut out for this line of work."**

It's important to note that a crime analyst has to be willing to work in the background and not always be in the limelight. The positive side is that a crime analyst plays a significant role in all of the big cases, but doesn't have to wear a bulletproof vest in 100-degree heat or direct traffic in the rain. "You can play cop without the danger," jokes Michelle.

HOW DO I BECOME A CRIME ANALYST?

EDUCATION

High School

While there are still a few law enforcement agencies that will hire crime analysts with only a high school diploma, it is becoming less common. Judy says, "Crime analysis used to be a field that a person could stray into, but most new analysts now are trained or educated specifically for the career."

There are plenty of ways that you can begin your own training and education now. First of all, get some exposure to the law enforcement community by volunteering at the local police department. Many towns have a Boy Scouts

Explorers program in which students (of both sexes) work and take mini-courses in law enforcement.

While you're finishing up high school, it pays to hone your writing skills. Michelle says, "You have to understand different styles of communicating so that you're able to write to the street cop and also to the city council." A good foundation in algebra will help with statistics classes in college. Moreover, take advantage of your school's computer lab, as a basic knowledge of computers, word processing, spreadsheets, and databases is important.

Postsecondary Training

The majority of agencies require a bachelor's degree for the position of crime analyst. Michelle earned her bachelor's degree in criminal justice, but it wasn't until her senior year of college that she actually learned about the field of crime analysis. "I had been trying to figure out how I wanted to use my degree. Then a senior seminar course in crime analysis was offered—the first of its kind. It sparked my interest and I began volunteering in my instructor's unit." When a job opened in the unit, Michelle applied and was hired. Judy, on the other hand, learned about crime analysis in high school and designed a personalized degree in criminology accordingly. Other excellent degrees to consider include statistics, criminal justice, computer science, and sociology.

Michelle, Judy, and Steven all agree that an internship during college is the best way to get a foot in the door and gain on-the-job experience. "Because of lean staffing, most units rely heavily on interns for support. The best thing is to contact a unit and talk with the crime analyst there," says Judy. She adds that a strong candidate for an internship would be organized, computer-literate, and have a basic understanding of statistics. In Judy's unit, interns initially begin by reading police reports, learning how to glean significant facts and patterns from them. "It's pretty exciting the first time a spark goes off and an intern says, 'Hey, there's a pattern here!'."

CERTIFICATION OR LICENSING

Currently, only California offers a formal, state-sponsored certification program for crime analysts. Steven was a key figure in establishing the certification program, which is supported by the California Department of Justice. After participating on several hiring panels, he says it became clear that some of the people applying for positions as crime analysts had solid experience in related areas, but could benefit from focused training in crime analysis.

The first university to offer the program was California State at Fullerton. Currently, four universities in the state offer it. To be certified, a person takes thirty-six to forty hours of courses. The curriculum focuses on crime analysis, criminal intelligence analysis, investigative analysis, and law enforcement research methods and statistics. Certification also requires prerequisites in criminal law, a competency in computer software, and four hundred hours of work experience, which is often earned volunteering at a police department.

WHO WILL HIRE ME?

The majority of crime analysts are employed by local and state law enforcement agencies. A great number are also hired by federal agencies such as the Federal Bureau of Investigation (FBI), the Customs Department, and the Department of Justice. In addition, some private security firms hire people with training in crime analysis.

While there's not a single, central clearinghouse for all crime analyst jobs, there are several places to look for listings. By becoming a member of the International Association of Crime Analysts (IACA), you'll receive a newsletter that includes job openings. Judy also advises finding out if there's a state association of crime analysts where you live and attending meetings, if possible. However, recent graduates would be best advised to be willing to move out of state if the job pickings are slim there.

The key to getting a job in the field is doing an internship in college (see "Postsecondary Training"). In the past six months, Judy has assisted several agencies who are hiring crime analysts for the first time. "It's not unusual for recent college graduates to be hired, but all of these people had done internships." Michelle adds that a new crime analyst would have a solid shot at finding a job in a larger, established unit where he or she could volunteer first, learning from someone with greater experience.

WHERE CAN I GO FROM HERE?

As a broad generalization, most crime analysts are not pushing and shoving to climb the career ladder. Since theirs is often a one- or two-person, non-hierarchical unit within an agency, they more likely chose crime analysis because they relish the nature of the work itself. Obviously, advancement possibilities depend largely on the size and structure of the agency a crime analyst works for. In larger agencies, there are sometimes senior analysts, supervising analyts, or crime analysis managers. Some of these positions require a master's degree.

More often, crime analysts set their sights on increasing the impact they have on the agency and community in which they work. Michelle says she sees herself staying in Santa Clara's unit and helping to establish a regional approach to crime analysis. "In the Bay Area, each agency has its own crime analysis unit and its own information system," she explains. "I'd like to work toward combining these resources and linking the individual systems."

WHAT ARE SOME RELATED JOBS?

The job of crime analyst falls under the wide umbrella of law enforcement careers. Related careers in this area include police officer, criminalist, FBI agent, crime scene evidence technician, state medical examiner, and forensic psychologist.

Related Jobs

Crime scene evidence technicians

Criminal intelligence analysts

Criminalists

Criminologists

FBI agents

Forensic psychologists

Investigative analysts

Police officers

State medical examiners

Two closely linked career opportunities are *criminal intelligence analyst* and *investigative analyst*. Criminal intelligence analysis involves the study of relationships between people, organizations, and events; it focuses on organized crime, money laundering, and other conspiratorial crimes.

Investigative analysis attempts to uncover *why* a person is committing serial crimes such as murder and rape. Getting into the field of investigative analysis (sometimes called "profiling") usually requires years of experience and additional education in psychology—as well as good instincts.

WHAT ARE THE SALARY RANGES?

The beginning salary for a crime analyst is about $24,000. With several years of experience, crime analysts can expect to earn $34,000 to $42,000, and the most experienced crime analysts earn about $60,000. Salaries tend to be higher in the East and West where crime analysis is more established as a profession and where the cost of living is higher. For instance, in California, a typical starting salary ranges from $27,000 to $40,000.

WHAT IS THE JOB OUTLOOK?

In the last five years, there has been a tremendous surge of interest in the field of crime analysis. One factor has been the emergence of community-oriented policing. This concept strives to get police officers out on the streets of their communities, rather than sitting at a desk. Michelle comments, "You want to put somebody behind a desk who actually wants to be there. The push in many departments is to 'civilianize' job functions so that police officers can work smarter, not harder." Crime analysis makes good use of the information that police officers collect on the streets. "With a limited number of officers, departments have to ask, 'What's the best use of their time?'" says Steven. "Good crime analysis helps to deploy officers in the right places at the right times."

// Good crime analysis helps to deploy officers in the right places at the right times."

The field is also growing because better software is becoming available. "Statistics are age-old," Steven says, "but doing them by hand was cumbersome. The newest technology—like sophisticated databases and geographic mapping systems—gives us increased capabilities."

U.S. News and World Report selected crime analyst as one of the "hot track" careers in 1996. The article states that the demand for this brand of technical analysis and computer know-how has increased tenfold in the past fifteen years.

While this growth trend is expected to continue, it's important to recognize that it is still a competitive job market. Those who want to become crime analysts should be willing to move to find an agency with a job opening. They should also bear in mind that police departments are historically more likely to lay off a civilian than a street officer.

Emergency Medical Technician

SUMMARY

DEFINITION
Emergency medical technicians *give immediate first aid treatment to sick or injured persons both at the scene and en route to the hospital or other medical facility. They also make sure that the emergency vehicle—an ambulance or a helicopter—is stocked with the necessary supplies and is in good operating condition.*

SALARY RANGE
$21,200 to $24,650 to $27,400

EDUCATIONAL REQUIREMENTS
High school diploma

CERTIFICATION OR LICENSING
Required

EMPLOYMENT OUTLOOK
Much faster than the average

HIGH SCHOOL SUBJECTS
Anatomy and Physiology
Computer science
English (writing/literature)
Health
Physical education

PERSONAL INTERESTS
Helping people: physical health/medicine
Helping people: protection

At 6:45 AM Kelly Richey clocks in, says hello to the EMTs going off duty, and goes to the Coke machine for her first Diet Coke of the day. It's half gone when the first call comes in, and fifteen minutes later she is inside a crumpled black Camaro, placing an oxygen mask on a critically injured teenager.

"Are you still in school?" she asks him as she works over him. "What grade? Senior?" She is trying to determine his level of consciousness, and she has to speak in a near-shout because the fire department is cutting the roof off the car while she works. As soon as the roof comes off, she and her co-worker must work quickly to get the patient out of the car and on the way to the hospital. He has injuries to the chest and both legs and is losing blood quickly. If he doesn't reach surgery within an hour, his chances for survival are greatly diminished.

In the ambulance, while her partner drives, Kelly continues to talk to the young man, taking his vital signs every few minutes. She calls the hospital emergency room to notify them that they have a serious trauma patient coming in. "We have a seventeen-year-old patient, conscious and alert," she begins. "Involved in a single vehicle accident. Patient has chest wounds and injuries to

47

both legs. Vital signs are stable. We have an ETA [estimated time of arrival] of five minutes."

At the hospital, she and her partner unload the patient and, after delivering him to the emergency staff, give a brief report to the doctor who will be on his case.

Kelly gets a blank "run report," and her second Diet Coke, and starts to document the first run of her day.

WHAT DOES AN EMERGENCY MEDICAL TECHNICIAN DO?

If you are sick or hurt, you usually go to a doctor; if you are very sick or hurt you may go to the emergency room of a local hospital. But what if you are alone and unable to drive, or you are too badly injured to travel without receiving medical treatment first? It often happens that an accident or injury victim needs on-the-spot help and safe, rapid transportation to the hospital. Emergency medical technicians are the ones who fill this need.

Emergency medical technicians, or EMTs, respond to emergency situations to give immediate attention to people who need it. Whether employed by a hospital, police department, fire department, or private ambulance company, the EMT crew functions as a traveling arm of the emergency room. While on duty, an EMT could be called out for car accidents, heart attacks, work-related injuries, or drug overdoses. He or she might help deliver a baby, treat the victim of a gunshot wound, or revive a child who has nearly drowned. In short, EMTs may find themselves in almost any circumstance that could be called a medical crisis.

Usually working in teams of two, EMTs receive their instructions from the emergency medical dispatcher, who has taken the initial

Lingo to Learn

Amkus cutter: *A hand-held rescue device, similar to scissors, used to free trapped victims by cutting through metal.*

Amkus rams: *A hand-held rescue device used to free trapped victims by pushing or pulling obstructions, such as dashboard and seats, away from the victim.*

Amkus spreader: *A hand-held rescue device used to free trapped victims by pulling crumpled metal apart.*

Backboard: *A long, flat, hard surface used to immobilize the spine in the case of neck or spinal injury.*

Cardiac arrest: *The complete stoppage of the heartbeat.*

Defibrillator: *An apparatus consisting of alternating currents of electricity, with electrodes to apply the currents to heart muscles in order to shock the muscles into operation. Requires the operator to interpret the heart rhythms and apply the shock at the proper time.*

Endotracheal intubation: *The insertion of a tube into the trachea, or windpipe, to provide a passage for the air, in case of obstruction.*

IV or intravenous: *Administered by an injection into the vein.*

call for help, and drive to the scene in an ambulance. (Some EMTs fly in helicopters to accident or trauma scenes and transport their patient by air to the hospital.) The dispatcher will remain in contact with the EMT crew through a two-way radio link. This allows the EMTs to relay important information about the emergency scene and the victims and to receive any further instructions, either from the dispatcher or from a medical staff member, if need be. Since they are usually the first trained medical help on the scene, it is very important that they be able to evaluate the situation and make good, logical judgments about what should be done in what order, as well as what should not be done at all. By observing the victim's injuries or symptoms, looking for medic alert tags, and asking the necessary questions, the EMTs determine what action to take and begin first aid treatment. Some more complicated procedures may require the EMT to be in radio contact with hospital staff who can give step-by-step directions.

The types of treatments an individual is able to give depend mostly on the level of training and certification he or she has completed. The first and most common designation is EMT-Basic. A basic EMT can perform CPR, control bleeding, treat shock victims, apply bandages, splint fractures, and perform automatic defibrillation, which requires no interpretation of EKGs. They are also trained to deal with emotionally disturbed patients and heart attack, poisoning, and burn victims. The EMT-Intermediate, which is the second level of training, is also prepared to start an IV, if needed, or use a manual defibrillator to apply electrical shocks to the heart in the case of a cardiac arrest. A growing number of EMTs are choosing to train for the highest level of certification—the EMT-Paramedic. With this certification, the individual is permitted to perform more intensive treatment procedures. Often working in close radio contact with a doctor, he or she may give drugs intravenously or orally, interpret EKGs, perform endotracheal intubation, and use more complex life-support equipment.

In the case where a victim or victims are trapped, EMTs first give any medical treatment, and then remove the victim, using special equipment such as the Amkus Power Unit. They may need to work closely with the police or the fire department in the rescue attempt.

If patients must be taken from the emergency scene to the hospital, the EMTs may place them on a backboard or stretcher, then carry and lift them into the ambulance. One EMT drives to the hospital, while the other monitors the passenger's vital signs and provides any further care. One of them must notify the hospital emergency room, either directly or through the dispatcher, of how

WHAT DOES AN EMT DO?, CONTINUED

many people are coming in and the type of injuries they have. They also may record the blood pressure, pulse, present condition, and any medical history they know, to assist the hospital.

Once at the hospital, the EMTs help the staff bring in the patient or patients, and assist with any necessary first steps of in-hospital treatment. They then provide their observations to the hospital staff, as well as information about the treatment they have given at the scene and on the way to the hospital.

Finally, each run must also be documented by the acting EMTs for the records of the provider. Once the run is over, the EMTs are responsible for restocking the ambulance, having equipment sterilized, replacing dirty linens, and making sure that everything is in order for the next run. For the EMT crews to function efficiently and quickly, they must make certain that they have all the equipment and supplies they need, and that the ambulance itself is clean, properly maintained, and filled with gas.

WHAT IS IT LIKE TO BE AN EMT?

Kelly Richey is a calm, soft-spoken twenty-nine-year-old woman who may save a life as a routine part of a day's work. For the past three years, she has worked for the hospital in an average-sized Indiana city as an EMT. Although her father had been an EMT for years, Kelly had no intention of working in Emergency Medical Services (EMS) when she first took the training course. "I just took the course for knowledge," she says. "I didn't really plan to do it as a job." However, during the training course clinicals, when she got the opportunity to actually go on runs, she changed her mind. "I just kind of got the fever," she says, laughing. "I decided it was something I wanted to do. I decided it was something I could do, and I thought if I can do this and I can save a life, I should maybe make this my profession."

Kelly's unit gives its EMTs the option of working two twenty-four-hour shifts or one eight-hour and two sixteen-hour shifts each week. Kelly has done both, but prefers the shorter hours, which she currently works. This number of hours is fairly common for employees of ambulance firms and hospitals. EMTs who work for fire and police departments may be scheduled for as many as fifty-six hours per week.

EMT work can be physically demanding. EMTs often work outside, in any type of weather, and most of their time on a run is spent standing, kneeling, bending, and lifting. It is also stressful and often emotionally draining. "I'm

EMTs on TV

*Not every job receives the media atten-
tion that the professions in the
emergency medical services
field do. The American television viewer can currently watch
ten to twelve full hours each
week of either fictional shows
based on hospital emergency
departments, or actual emergency personnel in action. The
only occupation that seems to
fascinate the public more is law
enforcement, with police shows
totalling over twenty-five hours
of air time weekly.*

pretty tired at the end of a shift," Kelly says. The sort of shift an EMT has depends almost entirely on how many and what type of calls come in. Some shifts are incredibly busy—up to fifteen runs, according to Kelly, although not all of those are emergency runs. Her ambulance is frequently dispatched to carry nursing home patients to and from the hospital for treatment, as well as to transport stable patients from the local hospital to the larger medical complex an hour away for scheduled surgeries. Other shifts are considerably slower, with maybe only seven runs in the entire sixteen hours.

At Kelly's hospital, the average length of a run is an hour and a half from dispatch until return to ready status. However, the location of the emergency and its seriousness greatly affect that time frame. There is a perception among many people that most calls involve life-or-death situations. That is not really the case, in Kelly's experience.

"On a monthly basis, only about 10 to 15 percent of my runs are actually life-threatening," she says. Other calls run the gamut from serious injury to cut fingers. "You wouldn't believe the stuff I've been called out for," Kelly says. "I've gotten calls for things you could put a Band-Aid on and go right about your business."

No matter what the call, the EMTs must respond. Each team of two has a certain area of the city that it is assigned to, but any team will take any call if the designated team for that area is already out. Kelly's hospital employs approximately seventy EMTs and paramedics, including several who work on a part-time schedule, and it staffs up to five ambulances during the busiest parts of the day.

All the EMTs in Kelly's unit are required to take a driver training program when they are hired, so they are all qualified to drive. Kelly says that she usually drives on every other run, alternating turns with her partner. The team schedule is set up in such a way that the same partners always work together. That way, they get used to working as a team and communicating with each other. Also, they are able to become accustomed to each other's techniques and work habits and are able to function more efficiently.

Not every emergency requires that a patient be taken to the hospital. If it isn't necessary, or if the patient refuses to go, the EMTs give treatment on-site

WHAT IS IT LIKE TO BE AN EMT?, CONTINUED

and return to await the next call. If a patient does need further attention, he or she is transported to the emergency room and unloaded by Kelly and her partner. The attending doctor is briefed on the case and the treatment. Whether a patient is transported or not, each run must be documented on a state-issued form called a run report.

Between calls, Kelly and her co-workers wait in the crewhouse. Complete with a kitchen, living room with TV, and two sleeping rooms, it has a comfortable, homey atmosphere. The ambulances are kept in an adjoining garage, and during each shift, if time allows, the crew is responsible for washing its vehicle and making sure it is fully stocked and ready to go. "Some people like to restock after every run," Kelly says. She and her partner prefer to take stock at the end of their shift and make sure everything is replaced. "That way you know you're leaving it in good shape for the shift coming on."

HAVE I GOT WHAT IT TAKES TO BE AN EMT?

EMTs regularly encounter situations that many people would find upsetting. Because they are faced with unpleasant scenes, crises, and even death, they need a certain emotional capability for coping. They must have stable personalities and be able to keep their heads in circumstances of extreme stress.

The stress level is the hardest thing about the job for Kelly. She also warns that the potential EMT must be able to deal with death. "There have been times when the family members have hung out in the ED [Emergency Department] after we brought patients in and that really gets to me," she says. "I feel like they're looking at me and saying, 'Why didn't you do more?' when I know I've done everything I could do." At Kelly's hospital, the staff has initiated a debriefing process to help EMTs work through a bad experience on a run. It's important that the EMT be able to cope with such bad experiences without suffering lasting negative results. The stress and the emotional strain can take its toll; there is a high turnover rate in the EMS field.

On the other hand, the job of EMT can be extremely fulfilling and rewarding. Kelly says that she tends to feel more confident and secure in all situations, just knowing she is trained to deal with many medical emergencies. But that's not the best part of it. "I like knowing I'm helping people," Kelly says. "I love

To be a successful emergency medical technician, you should:

Have a desire to serve people

Be emotionally stable and clearheaded

Have good manual dexterity and agility

Have strong written and oral communication skills

Be able to lift and carry up to 125 pounds

Have good eyesight and color vision

to know I may save someone's life." It's important for EMTs to have a willingness to help people, even when the patients they deal with are difficult and abusive. "Oh, I've been hit, kicked, spit on," laughs Kelly. "Drug overdoses and people with head injuries fight you a lot of the time." There is also always the possibility that a patient is infected with the AIDS virus, or another contagious disease. Although rubber gloves are commonplace, and the emergency staff at Kelly's hospital are now beginning to wear protective masks to cover their mouths, fear of disease is still something to consider. Regardless of the circumstances, the patient must be treated, so a genuine desire to serve is important to success in this field.

▲▲I like knowing I'm helping people. I love to know I may save someone's life."

Kelly's job is never routine. She enjoys the fact that she doesn't know from one day to the next, or even from one hour to the next, what she will be doing. "It's important to be flexible," she says. She also says it's important to be able to work closely with others. The partners have to rely heavily on each other and communicate easily and well to be a good emergency team. She describes the successful EMT as a person who can handle stress well, is confident in his or her abilities, communicates well, has physical strength and stamina, and wants to help others.

HOW DO I BECOME AN EMERGENCY MEDICAL TECHNICIAN?

All states offer EMT training programs consisting of 100 to 120 hours of training, usually followed by 10 hours of internship in a hospital emergency room. To be admitted into a training program, it is necessary to be 18 years old, a high school graduate, and hold a valid driver's license. Exact requirements vary slightly in different states and different courses.

EDUCATION

High School

A high school diploma, or its equivalent, is required for admission into the EMT training program. While most high school studies will not yield experience with emergency medical care, health classes may offer a good introduction to some of the concepts and terms used by EMTs. It may also be possible to take courses in first aid or CPR through the local Red Cross or other organizations. This sort of training can be valuable, giving the student advance preparation for the actual EMT program. Some science classes, such as anatomy, can also be helpful, in that students can become familiar with the human body and its various systems.

Driver's education is recommended as well for anyone who is interested in a career as an EMT. The ability to drive safely and sensibly in all different types of road conditions, and a firm knowledge of traffic laws is essential to the driver of an ambulance. English is a desirable subject for the potential EMT, since it is important to have good communication skills, both written and verbal, along with the capacity to read and interpret well. Finally, depending on what area of the country the potential EMT might work in, it might be very helpful to have a background in a foreign language, such as Spanish, to assist in dealing with patients who speak little or no English.

Postsecondary Training

For the high school graduate with a strong interest in the Emergency Medical Services, the next step is formal training. The standard training course was designed by the U.S. Department of Transportation and is often offered by police, fire, and health departments. It may also be offered by hospitals or as a nondegree course in colleges, particularly community colleges.

The program teaches EMTs-to-be how to deal with many common emergencies. The student will learn how to deal with bleeding, cardiac arrest, childbirth, broken bones, and choking. He or she will also become familiar with the specialized equipment used in many emergency situations, like backboards, stretchers, fracture kits, splints, and oxygen systems.

If in an area that offers several different courses, it might be a good idea for the student to research all the options, since certain courses may emphasize different aspects of the job. After completing the basic course, there are training sessions available to teach more specialized skills, such as removing trapped victims, driving an ambulance, or dispatching.

EMTs who have graduated from the basic program may later decide to work toward reaching a higher level of training in the EMS field. For example, the EMT-Intermediate course provides 35 to 55 hours of further instruction to allow the EMT to give more extensive treatment, and the EMT-Paramedic course offers an additional 750 to 2,000 hours of education and experience.

CERTIFICATION OR LICENSING

After the training program has been successfully completed, the graduate has the opportunity to work toward becoming certified or registered with the National Registry of Emergency Medical Technicians (NREMT) (see "Look to the Pros" at the end of this book). All states have some sort of certification requirement of their own, but many of them accept registration in NREMT in place of their own certification. Applicants should check the specific regulations and requirements for their state.

Whether registering with NREMT or being certified through a state program, the applicant for an EMT-Basic title will be required to take and pass a written examination, as well as a practical demonstration of skills. The written segment will usually be a multiple-choice exam of roughly 150 questions. In some states, EMTs work on a basic support vehicle for six months after passing the exam before certification is awarded.

The higher the level of training an EMT has reached, the more valuable he or she will become as an employee. EMTs who are registered at the Basic level may choose to work on fulfilling the requirements for an EMT-Intermediate certification. After the mandatory thirty-five to fifty-five hours of classroom training, as well as further clinical and field experience, another examination must be taken and passed. The EMT who wants to earn Paramedic status must already be registered as at least an EMT-Basic. He or she must complete a training program that lasts approximately nine months, as well as hospital and field internships, pass a written and practical examination, and work as a paramedic for six months before receiving actual certification.

All EMTs must renew their registration every one to two years, depending upon the state's requirement. In order to do so, they must be working at that time as an EMT, and meet the continuing education requirement, which is usually twenty to twenty-five hours of lectures and practical skills training.

LABOR UNIONS

Some EMTs may have the opportunity to join a union when they become employed, especially if they work for a municipal fire, police, or rescue department. EMTs with membership in a union pay weekly or monthly dues, and receive in return a package of services designed to improve working conditions, which include collective bargaining for pay and benefits, governmental lobbying, and legal representation.

WHO WILL HIRE ME?

Kelly was lucky when she started to look for a job as an EMT. "I just went to the hospital and filled out their application," she says. "They called me in for an interview and I got the job. I didn't even have to apply anywhere else." Not everyone will be lucky enough to get a job on the first try, but currently the statistics are in the favor of EMTs. The demand exceeds the number of persons trained to do the work. Most EMTs work for private ambulance services; municipal fire, police or rescue departments; and hospitals or medical centers. Also, there are many who volunteer, particularly in more rural areas, where there often are no paid EMTs at all. In fact, 70 percent of all ambulance service is provided by volunteers.

Because new graduates will be in heavy competition for full-time employment, it may be easier to break into the field on a part-time or volunteer basis. By beginning as a volunteer or part-timer, the new EMT can gain hours of valuable experience, which can be useful in landing a paid, full-time position later. The competition is also stiffer for beginning EMTs in the public sector, such as police and fire departments. Beginners may have more success in finding a position in a private ambulance company. There are also opportunities for work that lie somewhat off the beaten path. For example, many industrial plants have EMTs in their safety departments, and security companies sometimes prefer to hire EMTs for their staff. Most amusement parks and other public attractions employ EMTs in their first aid stations, and in many cities there are private companies that hire EMTs to provide medical services for rock concerts, fairs, sporting events, and other gatherings.

One good source of employment leads for an EMT graduate is the school or agency that provided his or her training. Job openings may sometimes be listed in the newspaper classifieds under "Emergency Medical Technician," "EMT," "Emergency Medical Services," "Ambulance Technician," "Rescue Squad," or "Health Care." It may be worthwhile for students nearing the end of their training course to subscribe to a local paper. Also, many professional journals and national and state EMS newsletters list openings. Finally, the National Association of Emergency Medical Technicians (NAEMT) prints each new member's resume in their monthly newsletter, upon request, so that prospective employers may see it (see "Look to the Pros" at the end of this book).

It is also a good idea for the graduate to apply directly to any local ambulance services, hospitals, fire departments, and police departments. The best approach is usually to send a current resume, complete with references, and a letter of inquiry. The letter should consist of a brief description of the applicant's situation and interests, and a request for an application. Most agencies have specific applications and employment procedures, so the resume and cover letter alone is not necessarily adequate. It is important to remember that most employers will accept applications to keep on file even if there is no specific job open at the time.

WHERE CAN I GO FROM HERE?

Kelly decided that she wanted to pursue more advanced levels of training shortly after she started working as an EMT. At present, she has already passed the paramedic training course and is getting ready to test for her certification. Eventually, she says, she might like to get into EMS education and train EMTs to do the job she does now.

Advancement Possibilities

Emergency medical services coordinators direct medical emergency service programs, coordinate emergency staff, maintain records, develop and participate in training programs for rescue personnel, cooperate with community organizations to promote knowledge of and provide training in first aid, and work with emergency services in other areas to coordinate activities and area plans.

Physician assistants work under the direction and responsibility of physicians to provide health care to patients: they examine patients; perform or order diagnostic tests; give necessary injections, immunizations, suturing, and wound care; develop patient management plans; and counsel patients in following prescribed medical regimens.

Training directors plan and oversee continuing education for rescue personnel, design and implement quality assurance programs, and develop and direct specialized training courses or sessions for rescue personnel.

Moving into the field of education and training is only one of several possible career options. For an EMT who is interested in advancement, usually the first move is to become certified as a paramedic. Once at that level, there are further opportunities in the area of administration. Moving into an administrative position usually means leaving field-work and patient care for a more routine office job. An EMT-Paramedic can pursue such positions as supervisor, operations manager, administrative director, or executive director of emergency services. Or, like Kelly, he or she may be interested in a career in education and training. Also, several new areas of specialization in EMS have recently received more emphasis. Quality control, safety and risk management, communications, and flight operations are some examples of these up-and-coming administrative areas.

Some EMTs move out of health care entirely and into sales and marketing of emergency medical equipment. Often, their experience and familiarity with the field make them effective and valuable salespersons. Finally,

WHERE CAN I GO FROM HERE?, CONTINUED

some EMTs decide to go back to school and become registered nurses, physicians, or other types of health workers. Kelly has seen EMTs take many different paths. "One girl who was a paramedic when I started at the hospital is a doctor now," she says, "so you can see how far you can go with it."

WHAT ARE SOME RELATED JOBS?

The job of EMT is similar to many other positions in the medical field in that there are very specific procedures and treatments that EMTs are trained and authorized to perform. The U.S. Department of Labor classifies Emergency Medical Technicians under the headings Occupations in Medicine and Health, Not Elsewhere Classified (DOT) and Patient Care (GOE). Also under this heading are people who work under the supervision of a doctor or registered nurse to assist in medical treatment in a variety of areas. The areas of specialization that these medical assistants, or aides, could work in include orthopedics, psychiatry, optometry, dentistry, occupational therapy, physical therapy, podiatry, and surgery.

WHAT ARE THE SALARY RANGES?

Related Jobs

Ambulance attendants

Birth attendants

Chiropractor's assistants

Dental assistants

First-aid attendants

Licensed practical nurses

Nurses' aides

Occupational therapy aides

Optometric assistants

Orderlies

Orthopedic assistants

Physical therapy aides

Podiatric assistants

Psychiatric aides

Surgical technicians

Salaries for emergency medical technicians have shown an increase of approximately 4 percent annually in recent years. Since the demand for qualified EMTs exceeds the supply at present, salaries will most likely continue to increase.

According to a 1997 salary survey published by the *Journal of Emergency Medical Services*, the average, overall salary for an EMT-Basic is approximately $24,670 per year. An EMT just starting out in the field can expect to make $21,200 on the average, and may eventually earn a salary in the high-twenties while still at Basic status. The average starting salary for an EMT-Intermediate is $23,250, while the average starting salary for an EMT-Paramedic is $25,200. The average top salaries for EMT-Intermediates and EMT-Paramedics are $30,265 and $34,240, respectively.

A significant factor in determining salary is whether the EMT is employed in the private or the public sector.

Typically, private ambulance companies and hospitals traditionally offer the lowest pay, while fire departments pay better. Geographical location is another significant factor. The average salary for an EMT-Basic varied from $22,050 in the Southeast, to $30,800 in the Northwest. And the percentage of employers offering life and medical insurance has declined over the last couple years. Now, about 82 percent of employers offer life insurance to the employee, and around 87 percent offer major medical insurance for the employee and their family. Other benefits commonly offered are uniform allowance, retirement or pension plans, and paid seminars and conferences.

WHAT IS THE JOB OUTLOOK?

Employment opportunities for EMTs are expected to grow much faster than the average for all occupations through the year 2006. One of the reasons for the overall growth is simply that the population is growing, thus producing the need for more medical personnel. Another factor is that the proportion of elderly people, who are the biggest users of emergency medical services, is growing in many communities. Finally, many jobs will become available because, as noted earlier, the EMT profession does have a high turnover rate.

The job opportunities for the individual EMT will depend partly upon the community in which he or she wishes to work. In the larger, more metropolitan areas, where the majority of paid EMT positions are found, the opportunities will probably be best. In many smaller communities, financial difficulties are causing many not-for-profit hospitals and municipal police, fire, and rescue squads to cut back on staff. Because of this, there are likely to be fewer job possibilities in the public sector. However, since many of the organizations suffering cutbacks opt to contract with a private ambulance company for service to their community, opportunities with these private companies may increase.

The trend toward private ambulance companies, which have historically paid less, is an important one, as it is likely to influence where the jobs will be found, as well as what the average pay is. One reason for the growth of the private ambulance industry is a health care reform concept called managed care. As health care costs increase, more Americans are leaving their private health care plans for "pool" systems, which provide health care for large groups. The reason this affects the EMT profession is that medical transportation is one of the major services typically contracted for by these pool systems, or managed care providers. As managed care gains popularity, there is a greater need for the private ambulance contractors.

Because of America's growing concern with health care costs, the person considering a career as an EMT should be aware of the fact that health care reforms may affect all medical professions to some extent. Also, as mentioned before, the increase and growth of private ambulance services will almost definitely change the face of the emergency services field. In looking at a future as an emergency medical technician, both of these factors are worth keeping in mind.

FBI Agent

SUMMARY

DEFINITION
Agents for the Federal Bureau of Investigation are responsible for investigating and enforcing 260 federal statutes that encompass organized crime, white-collar crime, public corruption, financial crime, government fraud, bribery, copyright matters, civil rights violations, bank robbery, extortion, kidnapping, air piracy, terrorism, foreign counterintelligence, interstate criminal activity, and fugitive and drug trafficking matters. Agents also conduct background investigations on certain federal government job applicants.

SALARY RANGE
$34,500 to $54,000 to $75,000

EDUCATIONAL REQUIREMENTS
Bachelor's degree

EMPLOYMENT OUTLOOK
About as fast as the average

HIGH SCHOOL SUBJECTS
Business
Computer science
English (writing/literature)
Mathematics
Psychology

PERSONAL INTERESTS
Business
Computers
Current events
Exercise/Personal fitness
Law
Photography
Reading/Books

Dale Weiss may have appeared to be on a vacation, basking in the sun on a sailboat off the coast of Aruba in 1986, but nothing could have been further from the truth. Dale, along with several other FBI agents, was actually working undercover to arrest three leaders of a Colombian drug cartel. She posed as a banker's assistant who was helping launder the drug lords' profits. She and other undercover agents lured the Colombians out onto a sailboat, saying they wanted to go watch a wind surfing contest. Fourteen miles into the ocean, in international waters, they were met by a U.S. Coast Guard ship with the FBI's elite Hostage Rescue Team on board. The drug lords, wearing only their bathing suits, were arrested.

Then Dale and her co-workers set sail back to Aruba, where a jet was waiting to whisk them back to safety in the United States. But the sailboat mast—where the agents' radio equipment was hidden—broke and brought the boat ten inches away from capsizing. With no life jackets on board and the boat about to overturn, the agents used wire cutters to clip the steel cables holding the mast to the boat. "My second or third thought was 'this only happens on TV. This doesn't happen in real life. The waves were so big and the wind was so horrible.' You could easily see your life go before you," Dale remembers.

61

Luckily, the agents discovered that the boat had a small engine that was used to navigate in and out of bays. They used the engine to navigate the twelve miles back to Aruba. "That was the closest to death I've been," Dale says.

WHAT DOES AN FBI AGENT DO?

Formed in 1908, the FBI has the broadest investigative authority of all federal law enforcement agencies. The agency leads long-term, complex investigations, while working closely with other federal, state, local, and foreign law enforcement and intelligence agencies.

An FBI special agent is faced with the challenge of investigating and upholding certain federal laws that come under the FBI's jurisdictions. Throughout their career, FBI agents conduct investigations on a variety of issues that are lumped into seven programs: federal employment applicant issues, civil rights, counterterrorism, financial crime, foreign counterintelligence, organized crime and drugs, and violent crimes and major offenders. FBI agents may be assigned to a wide range of investigations, unless they have specialized skills in a certain area. In short, agents are assigned to a case, conduct an investigation, and then submit a report of their findings to the U.S. Attorney's Office.

During an investigation, agents may use a vast network of communication systems and the bureau's crime detection laboratory to help them with their work. Agents may gather information with the help of the National Crime Information Center and the Criminal Justice Information Services Division. Once they have information, agents must make sure the facts and evidence are correct. FBI agents may discuss their findings with a U.S. attorney, who decides whether the evidence requires legal action. The Justice Department may choose to investigate the matter further, and the FBI agents may obtain a search warrant or court order to locate and seize property that may be evidence. If the Justice Department decides to prosecute the case, the agent may then obtain an arrest warrant.

Lingo to Learn

The Bureau: *The Federal Bureau of Investigation.*

Method of operation (M.O.): *The standard pattern that an individual typically uses to commit a crime.*

Profile: *A general description of a type of person who might commit a certain kind of crime. For example, the FBI creates profiles of serial killers and financial criminals.*

Special agent: *A government title for federal employees who investigate criminal violations.*

Street agent: *An FBI agent not in management who conducts investigations.*

Surveillance: *Following, observing, or listening to people.*

Wire tap: *Electronic surveillance over the telephone.*

With the goal of gathering information and reporting it, FBI agents may spend a considerable amount of time traveling or living in various cities. Their investigations often require the agent to interview people—witnesses, subjects, or suspects—and search for different types of records. Agents may set up a stakeout to watch a place or person. Special agents may also work with paid informants. Sometimes agents testify in court about their investigations or findings. If enough incriminating evidence is found, FBI agents conduct arrests or raids of various types. Agents must carry firearms while on duty, and they usually carry their bureau identification badge. Most of the time they wear everyday business suits or other appropriate attire—not uniforms.

Some agents with specialized skills may work specific types of investigations, such as fraud or embezzlement. *Language specialists*—who can be employed as special agents or support personnel—may translate foreign language over a wiretap and tape recordings into English. The FBI also employs agents specializing in areas such as chemistry, physics, metallurgy, or computers. *Laboratory specialists* analyze physical evidence like blood, hair, and body fluids, while others analyze handwriting, documents, and firearms. Agents working for the FBI's Behavioral Science Unit track and profile serial murderers, rapists, and other criminals committing patterned violent crimes.

Agents often work alone, unless the investigation is particularly dangerous or requires more agents. However, FBI agents do not investigate local matters—only federal violations that fall within their jurisdiction. The agents' work can be discussed only with other bureau employees, which means they cannot discuss investigations with their families or friends.

The FBI's headquarters is made up of nine divisions and four offices. The FBI also operates fifty-six field offices, about four hundred resident agencies, four specialized field installations, and twenty-three foreign liaison posts. FBI agents must be willing to be reassigned at any point in their career.

WHAT IS IT LIKE TO BE AN FBI AGENT?

The life of an FBI agent is unpredictable. Agents may go into their offices in the morning and spend the day searching through records or watching a suspect. Or, they may be called out for a number of different emergency assignments. "There's no typical day for any FBI agent due to the hundreds of duties and tasks we have," Dale Weiss says. And she should know. After nineteen years as an FBI agent, the forty-three-year-old says the law enforcement dramas on television do not come close to portraying the true excitement and danger the job entails.

During her investigations, Dale has encountered situations ranging from hilarious to disgusting. She remembers an incident in New York City, where she was investigating city employees who were accepting bribes from companies and allowing them to dump illegal hazardous waste. Besides dangerous materials such as asbestos, the employees were accepting hazardous medical waste—and Dale was watching. One pile of medical waste was three stories high. "Every time a new truckload would come in, a number of heroin addicts would come out of the bushes. They would come running in and rummage through (the waste) to find used syringes," she remembers. "At one spot, I remember, body parts were being dropped by the dump trucks as they unloaded. You see some pretty grim things."

History of the FBI

The FBI was founded in 1908 to serve as the investigative arm of the U.S. Department of Justice. In the early years, agents investigated federal violations such as bankruptcy frauds, antitrust crime, and neutrality violations. During World War I, the bureau began investigating espionage, sabotage, sedition, and draft violations. In 1932, kidnapping became a federal crime, and the 1934 U.S. Congress gave special agents the authority to make arrests and carry firearms. After World War II, the FBI began conducting background security investigations for government agencies, as well as probes into internal security matters for the executive branch of the federal government. The 1960s brought civil rights and organized crime to the forefront for the FBI, and the '70s and '80s focused on counterterrorism, financial crime, drugs, and violent crimes.

Besides seeing dire sights, FBI agents may also experience difficult situations first-hand. "I remember having to lay out in a cornfield in Iowa all night long and having bugs crawling all over me," Dale says.

The work can be intense and sometimes draining. While all agents must work a minimum of fifty hours a week—sometimes seventy hours a week—they may also have to work nights or go for extended periods of time with little or poor sleep. A good example occurred in Jordan, Montana, when the FBI was dealing with the antigovernment Freemen group in 1995. "We had hundreds of agents up there and accommodations were very poor. Our SWAT team was sleeping in mangers in the county barn for a while," Dale says.

Another drawback to the job is, of course, the physical hazards it presents. Dale has risked her life on the job, as have many of her co-workers. So far, she has known six agents who died in the line of duty. They were killed in different ways, several in car accidents, one in a shootout. "Danger is a problem. Most agents who go into this are told that they may risk their life, that they have to carry a gun, and may have to shoot someone," she says.

Despite the long hours and sometimes extreme conditions, many agents find the job fun and intriguing. "You never know what will happen," Dale says. "You may be interviewing the governor of your state one minute, and the next, meeting a dirty bank robber or a suspect in a case who doesn't even have a place to live. It's quite fascinating." Agents are constantly meeting new people, and the work can turn out to be very rewarding.

▮▮I think most agents are in this business because they want to make the world a better place. You can see actual, physical changes that you can make and that's very satisfying."

The outcome of the job was the reason Dale became interested in the FBI. "I think most agents are in this business because they want to make the world a better place. You can see actual, physical changes that you can make and that's very satisfying, whether it's putting handcuffs on somebody or sending a criminal to prison or seeing a victim get back money," she says. The rewarding moments of the job are usually shared with other agents; the relationships FBI agents build with their co-workers are often strong and close, due to the life-and-death severity of their duties. "The FBI itself is a big family. When one employee gets hurt or has a problem, everyone chips in and tries to help out," she says.

HAVE I GOT WHAT IT TAKES TO BE AN FBI AGENT?

To be an FBI agent, you must be between the ages of twenty-three and thirty-seven. You must be a citizen of the United States or the Northern Mariana Islands. Candidates must be available for assignment anywhere in the FBI's headquarters or field offices and possess a valid driver's license.

FBI agents must have the ability to use tact and good judgment, especially in challenging and quickly evolving situations. They need strong coping skills to deal with sudden events or crises. Agents must also have good observation skills and the ability to conduct an investigation in a discerning and efficient manner. They must be willing to relocate and be on call twenty-four hours a day, every day of the year—even when they are on vacation.

Since they work every day with different types of people, FBI agents should enjoy meeting and dealing with people. And it helps to have a broad knowledge of the world, Dale says. "You never know when you might use a skill you possess. Agents with art degrees have helped investigate international art theft rings." People who read a lot also make good agents, because they are curious and usually have more knowledge in general. Agents also need to have good writing and speaking skills to carry them through court appearances. "Honesty and integrity are of premier importance. We have to be above reproach," she says.

FBI agents must also be in excellent health to pass a physical exam. Applicants will be disqualified if they have a physical condition that interferes with firearm use, raids, or defensive tactics. If you are considering the job, you cannot be color-blind, and you must have uncorrected vision of no less than 20/200 in each eye without glasses, corrected to 20/20 in one eye and no less than 20/40 in the other.

In addition, you may be disqualified if you have been convicted of a felony or major misdemeanor, used illegal drugs, or fail to pass a polygraph test or drug test. "Generally speaking, you have got to have a clean record," Dale says. "Thirty to forty people that have known you will likely be interviewed during your background investigations."

To be a successful FBI agent, you should:

Be between the ages of twenty-three and thirty-seven and a citizen of the United States or the Northern Mariana Islands

Be in excellent physical health

Have strong writing and speaking skills

Have the ability to use tact and good judgment, especially in challenging and quickly evolving situations

Be willing to relocate and be on call twenty-four hours a day

Enjoy meeting and dealing with people

HOW DO I BECOME AN FBI AGENT?

Contact the applicant coordinator or special agent recruiter of the FBI field office nearest you to request an application or information about career opportunities. Your local telephone directory should list the telephone number and the address of the field office closest to you.

High School

A high school diploma, or its equivalent, is required. The FBI does not recommend specific courses for high school students. Rather, the bureau encourages students to do the best work they can. Since FBI agents perform a variety of work, numerous academic disciplines are needed.

Postsecondary Training

Candidates must be graduates from a four-year resident program at a college or university that is accredited by one of the six regional accrediting bodies of the Commission on Institutions of Higher Education. Applicants with a law degree must have received that degree from a state-accredited, resident school, and their undergraduate work must be from a resident school also accredited from the commission.

The bureau offers entrance programs in law, accounting, language, and diversified. The law school program accepts law school graduates with two years of undergraduate work. The accounting school program accepts accounting graduates who have also passed the Uniform Certified Public Accountant Examination, or provided proof from their undergraduate school that they are academically eligible to sit for the exam. The language program accepts graduates who fluently speak a foreign language for which the bureau has a current need. The diversified program accepts graduates who possess three years full-time work experience, or an advanced degree and two years work experience.

Applicants with law or accounting degrees are especially valued by the FBI. Since agents investigate violations of federal law, a law degree may give applicants an appreciation and understanding of the Federal Rules of Criminal Procedure. Plus, a law degree should help agents identify the elements of a criminal violation and collect the necessary evidence for successful prosecution. Since FBI agents trace financial transactions and review and analyze complex accounting records, an accounting degree will likely help agents document evidence and reveal sophisticated financial crimes.

FBI agent applicants are required to pass a written exam. Those passing the exam will then be interviewed based on their overall qualifications and the needs of the bureau. Applicants being considered for employment must undergo a thorough background investigation, polygraph test, and a urinalysis to determine illegal drug usage.

If appointed to the position of an FBI special agent, new hires train for fifteen weeks at the FBI Academy in Quantico, Virginia. Classroom hours are spent studying academic and investigative subjects, and agent trainees also focus on physical fitness, defensive tactics, and firearms training. Emphasis is placed on developing investigative techniques, as well as skills in interviewing, interrogation, and gathering intelligence information. Agent trainees are tested on their defensive tactics, firearms and weapon handling, physical fitness, and arrest techniques. They must also pass academic exams and obey certain rules and regulations during the training. If the trainees pass the tests at the academy and receive their credentials, they become special agents and are assigned to serve a two-year probationary period at an FBI field office.

INTERNSHIPS

Each summer the FBI offers the Honors Internship Program to a select group of outstanding undergraduate and graduate students. The program allows qualified participants to spend the summer working for the FBI in Washington, DC, and learn about the bureau's operations and career opportunities. The program is extremely competitive and selects only individuals with strong academic credentials, outstanding character, a high degree of motivation, and the ability to represent the FBI upon return to their campus.

To be considered, undergraduate candidates must be enrolled in their junior year when they apply to the program, and graduate students must be enrolled full-time at a college or university. Applicants must have a cumulative grade point average of at least 3.0 and be returning to their campus after the program. All candidates must be U.S. citizens.

To apply for the program, contact the FBI field office closest to your campus for an application. You must complete and return an FD-646a application form, current academic transcript, personal resume, recent photograph, written recommendation from the appropriate dean or department head, and a five-hundred-word essay expressing your interest in the program. Application packages should be submitted before November 1.

Qualified candidates are interviewed and each field office nominates candidates to the FBI Personnel Division by December 1. A headquarters selection committee chooses the finalists, who must then pass an extensive background investigation and drug-screening test. The director of the FBI gives final approval for program participants. Selections are based on academic achievement, area of study, life or work experiences, and interest in law enforcement. Because of the bureau's long-term needs, students with skills and education in the areas of engineering, computer science, foreign languages, political science, law, accounting, and the physical sciences receive special consideration.

Once selected, FBI interns are assigned to a headquarters division based on their academic discipline, potential contribution to the division, and the needs of the FBI. Interns work side by side with FBI agents and learn about the inner operations of the bureau. Undergraduate interns are paid at the government's GS-6 grade level—about $23,300 annually in 1997—and graduate interns are paid at the GS-7 level—about $25,900 annually in 1997. Interns' travel expenses to and from the Washington, DC program are reimbursed by the FBI.

WHO WILL HIRE ME?

The FBI hires on a continual basis, although some years it does not hire any new agents. When the bureau is hiring, they advertise in newspapers, postings, and the Internet.

Dale applied to the FBI after she graduated from college, but since she was too young and didn't have enough work experience, she was not accepted until two years later. She worked for a couple of years as a consumer fraud investigator with a state district attorney office and was then accepted into the academy in 1978. Since women weren't allowed to serve as agents for the bureau until 1972, Dale was one of the first forty female FBI agents.

After completing the training at the academy, her first assignment was in Omaha, Nebraska, and then Des Moines, Iowa. She worked in Iowa for four years, investigating almost all types of federal violations. She mainly performed "reactive work," like investigating bank robberies, interstate transportation of stolen property, and financial crimes.

If you are interested in working for the FBI, write to the applicant coordinator at the FBI field office nearest you. The bureau will send you information on existing vacancies, requirements for the positions, how to file applications, and locations where examinations will be given.

WHERE CAN I GO FROM HERE?

Dale says she's happy with her current job at the FBI: she's still considered a street agent, but she is also the FBI's training coordinator for the Utah-Idaho-Montana region. She teaches or arranges training seminars regarding subjects such as how to work with the media, interview interrogation, and others. Occasionally, if a case comes up that requires her expertise, she will be called out to investigate it. "My current job is not as exciting as constantly investigating cases. But on the other hand, it's something that you want to do once you obtain a certain amount of experience. You want to teach people how to do the job," she says.

FBI promotions are awarded mainly on performance, rather than seniority. All administrative and supervisory jobs are filled from within the ranks by agents who have demonstrated they are able to handle more responsibility. Some FBI agents climb the ladder to become higher-grade administrators and supervisors. For example, an agent may become an inspector, field supervisor, or special agent in charge of a field office. Agents may also be assigned to the FBI headquarters, or they may become bureau supervisors, unit and section chiefs, and division heads. Agents may retire after twenty years of service, and after the age of fifty; mandatory retirement is required at the age of fifty-seven.

Dale is not sure when she will retire. But when the time comes, she plans to volunteer her time to teach investigative work for a small organization that otherwise would not be able to afford law enforcement instruction. Retired FBI agents often become consultants, teachers, attorneys, and private investigators. Many retirees also work for security departments of large corporations.

Advancement Possibilities

Assistant Special Agents in Charge *supervise specific programs—such as those designed to deal with financial crime and domestic terrorism—and special agents.*

Special Agents in Charge *oversee a field office or program area, report to the FBI headquarters, and are usually in charge of at least one hundred people.*

Supervisory Special Agents *are supervisors of a squad who ensure all procedures are complied with and the squad has everything they need to conduct their job. (A squad includes the agents and sometimes support employees needed to work a specific violation.)*

WHAT ARE SOME RELATED JOBS?

The U.S. Department of Labor classifies FBI agents under the heading Investigating Occupations. Also under this heading are private investigators, fire wardens, customs patrol officers, deputy sheriffs, U.S. marshals, detectives, fish and game wardens, narcotics investigators, police officers, state highway patrol officers, and regional wildlife agents. FBI agents are also classified with public service police officers, border guards, and fingerprint classifiers.

Besides the special agent position, the FBI hires people for jobs listed in four categories: professional, administrative, technical, and clerical. Professional positions include attorneys, chemists, personnel psychologists,

Related Jobs

Border guards

Customs patrol officers

Deputy sheriffs

Detectives

Fingerprint classifiers

Fish and game wardens

Narcotics investigators

Police officers

Private investigators

Regional wildlife agents

State highway patrol officers

U.S. marshals

and contract specialists. Administrative positions include intelligence research specialists, computer specialists, management analysts, and language specialists. Technical positions include evidence technicians, accounting technicians, and computer operators. Clerical positions include secretaries, personnel assistants, office automation assistants, and file clerks.

WHAT ARE THE SALARY RANGES?

New FBI agents start out at the federal government's GS-10 level—approximately $34,900 in 1997, depending on where the agent lives. They can receive up to 10 hours of overtime pay each week, but overtime pay is 25 percent of regular pay. Salaries are increased slightly for agents living in high cost-of-living areas such as New York, Los Angeles, and Miami. FBI agents can earn within-grade pay increases upon satisfactory job performance, and grade increases may be earned as the agent gains experience through good job performance. FBI agents in nonsupervisory positions can reach the GS-13 grade—about $54,000 in 1997. After 19 years, Dale is at a GS-13, step 7, which earns her about $64,000 in Salt Lake City. Agents that move into management positions can earn a GS-15 salary—about $75,000. Some agents then move into a different employment category called the Senior Executive Service, where they make more than $100,000 annually working for the FBI. Benefits include paid vacation, health and life insurance, retirement, sick leave, and job-related tuition reimbursement.

WHAT IS THE JOB OUTLOOK?

Most FBI agents make a career out of their service to the bureau. As a result, employee turnover is relatively low, with vacancies occurring because of retirement, death, or promotions from within the bureau. However, new positions are created as the bureau expands. Competition is keen for the jobs, but openings do occur regularly, and the FBI encourages qualified and interested people to submit applications.

WHAT IS THE JOB OUTLOOK?, CONTINUED

"With the growing population, there is no doubt there is going to be a growing amount of federal crime and I think the FBI will increase the number of agents and employees, in general," Dale says. "Unfortunately, the FBI, as well as any area of law enforcement, will always have jobs. There is always going to be crime."

Since the FBI sends agents wherever they are needed, it doesn't matter what part of the country an agent-trainee comes from. Plus, Dale says, it's hard to predict what areas the FBI will need help with, because crime is trendy and constantly changing. However, at the moment she sees computer crime and health care fraud as possible areas the FBI may need people to work in. Dale doesn't expect technology to ever outdate her profession. Rather, she believes innovations will be used to help agents at their job, for example, with new types of surveillance equipment.

Firefighter

SUMMARY

DEFINITION

Professional firefighters serve the public by protecting citizens and their property from fire and its effects. Firefighters also respond to other types of emergencies including emergency medical incidents, hazardous material spills, and various types of rescue calls.

ALTERNATIVE JOB TITLES

Smoke jumper
Wildland firefighter

SALARY RANGE

$27,800 to $37,000 to $40,000

EDUCATIONAL REQUIREMENTS

High school diploma

CERTIFICATION OR LICENSING

Required

EMPLOYMENT OUTLOOK

About as fast as the average

HIGH SCHOOL SUBJECTS

Anatomy and Physiology
Chemistry
Computer science
Physics
Speech

PERSONAL INTERESTS

Helping people: personal service
Helping people: physical health/medicine
Helping people: protection

It's about 10:00 AM on a sunny August day when the call comes in: Smoke and flames are pouring out of the Howard Apartments in Missoula, Montana. The firefighters quickly don their heavy, fire-resistant bunkers, jump onto the fire engines, and head downtown. Thirty-year-old Tony Cate is among them.

His adrenaline pumps as he arrives on the scene, less than two minutes after the call came in. Heavy, black smoke rushes out of a third-story window. People lean out the windows yelling for help.

Two firefighters grab a heavy fire hose and drag it up the stairs to the burning third-story apartment. The carpet is already melting from the intense heat in the room. Some firefighters hoist ladders to rescue the people hanging from the windows. Tony and several other firefighters connect their masks to their air tanks and run into the building to get people out. Smoke fills the corridors, which have already heated to about 200 degrees near the floor and even hotter near the ceiling. A tenant in his sixties, who is trying to put out the fire with a fire extinguisher, is overcome by smoke. The firefighters rescue him from the building and perform CPR until the man is taken to the hospital.

The crew is able to contain and extinguish the fire fairly quickly, but the man dies. Then the firefighters begin the laborious job of removing the charred debris. Later they learn the fire was started by a five-year-old playing with matches.

WHAT DOES A FIREFIGHTER DO?

Professional firefighters must be ready in seconds to jump on a fire engine, drive to a fire, and then work to protect and rescue people, extinguish the fire, and save personal property. While fire fighting can be rewarding, it is one of the most dangerous professions around. Nearly 40 percent of all professional fire-fighters are injured every year. Every day firefighters risk their lives by responding to fire calls, as well as emergency medical requests, hazardous material spills, and various types of rescue calls. Besides the danger of fire, firefighters may jeopardize their own safety through exposure to toxic materials and contagious diseases such as tuberculosis, hepatitis, and HIV.

During fire suppression calls, firefighters are required to connect hose lines to hydrants, operate pumps, apply water or other extinguishing agents through hose lines and nozzles, and position ladders. firefighters also ventilate smoke-filled areas, operate heavy equipment, salvage building contents, rescue victims, and administer emergency medical care. After the fire is extinguished, firefighters remove the debris (they call it "overhaul") and often remain at the scene to ensure the fire does not start again.

When responding to a fire call, firefighters wear protective gear to prevent their hands and bodies from being burned. They may also use a self-contained breathing apparatus. Once the fire is extinguished, fire investigators or fire marshals may examine the site to determine the cause of the fire, especially if they suspect the fire was set intentionally, or if it resulted in injury or death.

Lingo to Learn

Fire point: *The temperature at which a flammable liquid emits enough vapors to sustain a fire ignited by an outside source.*

Flash over: *The temperature at which everything in a room reaches ignition temperature and spontaneously ignites.*

Flash point: *The temperature at which a flammable liquid emits enough vapors to briefly ignite when an outside ignition source is present.*

Ignition temperature: *The temperature at which a substance ignites without an outside ignition source.*

Water hammer: *The potentially damaging surge of water that results when the flow of water though fire hose or pipe is suddenly stopped. Can often be heard as a distinct sharp clank.*

Besides responding to fire suppression calls, most professional firefighters are trained as emergency medical technicians or paramedics to provide emergency medical care to ill or injured people. firefighters carry equipment such as cardiac defibrillators and life-saving medication, and they are trained to stabilize and transport sick or hurt people to hospitals.

Responding to fires and emergency medical calls are the most visible aspects of working as a firefighter, but the job entails other duties as well. firefighters are also responsible for dealing with incident command, hazardous materials, high angle rescue, water and ice rescue, wildland fires, fire prevention, fire investigations, communications, fire education, and community relations. In addition, they may be required to respond to environmental emergencies such as earthquakes, floods, and blizzards. Most professional firefighters educate the people in their community on the hazards of fire, and teach school children about the dangers of fire and the correct reactions to emergency situations.

In addition, some firefighters are trained to prevent fires by inspecting buildings for trash, chemicals, and hazardous conditions that may result in a fire. Inspectors check exit routes, the storage and use of flammable and combustible materials, overcrowding of public places, and the improper use of equipment or materials in all types of buildings to ensure local fire and building codes are being met and that hazardous conditions are not present. Faulty or damaged wiring and inadequate alarm systems may also pose fire hazards. Substandard conditions are reported to the property owner and their correction is required by law. Fire inspectors may also present fire prevention programs to local school and civic groups.

When firefighters are not on a call or dealing with the public, they clean and maintain their equipment to keep it in immaculate condition. Mechanical equipment is polished and lubricated, water hoses are washed, and personal protective gear is kept in excellent condition. firefighters also attend training courses and conduct practice drills to improve their skills and knowledge of fire fighting and emergency medical techniques. Down time is often spent studying for examinations, which usually influence firefighters' promotional opportunities. Many firefighters read professional journals to keep abreast of technological developments and administrative practices and procedures.

Since many firefighters live at the fire station during their shift—for up to twenty-four hours at a time—those on duty perform housekeeping and cleaning duties. Chores include cooking meals, cleaning bathrooms, and making beds. Many fire stations offer exercise facilities, which are available to firefighters to help them increase and maintain their physical abilities.

While the vast majority of professional firefighters work for municipal fire departments, industrial plants also hire professional firefighters to prevent and suppress fires. In addition, airports hire firefighters to prevent and combat fires, and also save passengers and crew members in the event of a crash or accident. Other professionals work for the federal or state government as wildland firefighters, often parachuting out of airplanes to get to inaccessible forest fires. These parachuting firefighters are often called *smoke jumpers.*

WHAT IS IT LIKE TO BE A FIREFIGHTER?

As a fire fighter in Missoula, Montana, Tony's primary goals are to protect people, save property, and ease the pain and suffering that result from emergency situations such as fires, car accidents, and chemical spills. When he gets to the fire station, he and his co-workers check and clean all of their equipment. Tanks must be filled with water, gas, or air, and hoses must be loaded on the trucks properly, ready to extinguish fires. The firefighters inspect and stock medical equipment, ensuring the trucks are equipped with items such as oxygen, suctions, defibrillators, and extraction gear. The equipment check usually takes about an hour, and then the firefighters begin their housekeeping chores. Each day they mop floors, scrub toilets, vacuum carpets, and wash dishes—the typical chores needed to keep the house-like atmosphere in order.

> **"The one caveat is everything comes to a halt as emergency calls come in. We drop whatever we are doing to respond to calls."**

Around 10:30 AM, the firefighters practice proactive emergency response drills. They may drive through an area of the town, planning the best routes to take should an emergency occur in that area. They walk through larger buildings and possible hazardous areas that could be the site of a future call for help. From noon to 1 PM, the firefighters break for lunch, and then spend the rest of the afternoon training, practicing, or learning new emergency response techniques and procedures. Then 4 to 6 PM is set aside for personal time, and most of the firefighters take the opportunity to exercise in the on-site facility, or study for the numerous exams coming up.

"The one caveat is everything comes to a halt as emergency calls come in. We drop whatever we are doing to respond to calls," Tony says. "Obviously those don't come at half hour intervals throughout the day. There are some days when we might have one or two calls the whole day for the whole city. Other days it seems like we're going on calls all day long."

The Missoula Fire Department responded to four thousand calls in 1996, 60 percent of which were medical calls. While their day is mapped out, rarely does it work out according to the schedule. Usually the firefighters respond to at least one call a day. "It seems like we probably go on at least one car accident call a day," says Tony.

The History of Fire Fighting in America

The first permanent fire fighting company was formed in Philadelphia in 1736 by Benjamin Franklin, followed by New York in 1737, and then the remaining colonies. Growth during the nineteenth century led to an increased need for professional firefighters and proper equipment, and many cities suffered devastating fires as a result of conditions such as the lack of a sufficient water supply, crowded conditions, and poor building techniques. In 1871, the Great Chicago Fire killed 250 people, destroyed practically all of the city, and caused $196 million in property losses. Fire prevention week, scheduled in October of each year, commemorates the Great Chicago Fire.

In Missoula, firefighters work four shifts totaling forty-eight hours every eight days. Depending on local conditions, professional firfighters are required to work between forty and fifty-six hours a week. To ensure crews are available at all hours of the day, professional firefighters work in shifts—most often the twenty-four hour tour or the split shift. The twenty-four hour shift requires firefighters to work twenty-four hours on duty followed by either forty-eight or seventy-two hours off. The split shift requires firefighters to work either nine-hour days and fifteen-hour nights, or ten-hour days and fourteen-hour nights. After each set of day shifts, a fire fighter is given about seventy-two hours off, and after each set of night shifts, a fire fighter is given forty-eight hours off.

Whatever the shift, the work of a firefighter can be extremely dangerous. According to the U.S. Fire Administration, nearly one hundred firefighters die in service to their communities each year, and about one hundred thousand suffer injuries, many of which are very serious. Firefighters work in all kinds of weather and conditions, often battling heat, flames, smoke, gases, chemicals, poisonous fumes, and the risk of building collapse.

HAVE I GOT WHAT IT TAKES TO BE A FIREFIGHTER?

Above all, firefighters must be committed to their job of protecting and saving lives and property. Without that commitment, the dangerous conditions and long hours turn many people away from the career. Firefighters should also possess courage, confidence, knowledge, physical agility, and endurance, but they also need compassion and adaptability to be successful.

Firefighters must make quick decisions in emergencies, so initiative and good judgment are important. Because firefighters eat, sleep and work closely together under stressful and dangerous conditions, they should also be reliable, able to get along well with others, and comfortable working with a team. Leadership qualities are vital for officers, who direct the activities of fire fighting crews, and establish and maintain discipline and efficient operations.

HAVE I GOT WHAT IT TAKES?, CONTINUED

Tony says firefighters need self confidence. "Once you've been given the tools to do the job through training and experience, you need to know that you can do the job," he says. It doesn't do anybody any good if they're relying on you and you have self-doubt, and that self-doubt comes out in your performance. Patients will pick up on that. If you're insecure about what you're doing to them, they're going to feel insecure about what you're doing to them."

To be a successful firefighter, you should:

Be committed to protecting and saving lives and property

Have courage, confidence, physical agility, and endurance

Be able to make quick decisions in emergencies

Be able to get along well with others and be comfortable working as a member of a team

Have good communication skills

Be able to deal with tragedy and death

He is also convinced good communication skills are vital to the field. Firefighters need to find out pertinent information from different types of people ranging from an elderly fire victim to a toddler injured in a car accident. Another important characteristic for firefighters is the ability to deal with tragedy and death. "Certain life experience is necessary," Tony says. "You have to be able to maturely handle it."

HOW DO I BECOME A FIREFIGHTER?

EDUCATION

High School

Virtually every fire department requires applicants to possess a high school degree or its equivalent. When Tony was in high school, he planned on becoming a wildlife biologist and took classes in science and math. He didn't decide to become a firefighter until he was in college, but says many of his high school classes helped him prepare for the career.

Classes pertaining to human anatomy, physics, and chemistry are helpful, and Tony also recommends students learn about computers, which are becoming more and more useful for fire departments. Some departments are already relying on computerized systems to help them determine the best route to a fire. Some fire departments use the Internet to collect a variety of information on topics ranging from the weather to other departments' procedures. In the future, computer simulations may show firefighters the best method to extinguish specific fires.

Considering the wide variety of tasks firefighters perform, Tony believes most high school classes are beneficial in some manner. For example, auto shop could help firefighters maintain fire trucks, home economics would help with meal preparation, and theater or drama classes may help with public fire education presentations, such as puppet shows.

Postsecondary Training

Generally people become professional firefighters between the ages of eighteen and thirty-five. Most fire departments require applicants to be U.S. citizens and have a driver's license; some departments require candidates to be residents of the community in which they intend to serve.

Applicants for most municipal fire fighting jobs are required to take written and physical examinations. Candidates who pass those exams are usually interviewed and then ranked according to their scores. Then, when an opening comes up at a fire department, the applicants with the best test scores usually have the best chance of getting hired.

Applicants must also meet height and weight requirements. A drug test and security background check may be required, as well as a preexisting medical conditions exam and psychological screening.

Although not required, a growing number of candidates have a four-year college degree when they apply for a fire fighting job. Some departments require applicants to attend a fire fighting training program at a vocational/technical school or a two-year college degree program that teaches fire protection and control.

That's what Tony did. After fighting wildland fires to pay for his college, he decided he wanted to become a professional municipal firefighter. So he earned an associate's degree in fire science from Rio Hondo College in Southern California. As part of the program, Tony also became a certified emergency medical technician, a requirement for applicants by some fire departments. In addition, some applicants are required to receive hazardous materials training, and military applicants may be required to show they have been trained in fire fighting techniques.

Fire fighting testing is extremely rigorous and competitive. On average, it can take five years or more to get hired on a full-time permanent basis. For each position available, there are generally between one thousand and three thousand applicants.

CERTIFICATION OR LICENSING

Professional firefighters are certified for fire fighting according to standards established by their municipalities. Generally new hires in large fire departments train for several weeks at the department's training center. New firefighters are taught in classrooms and in the field, and study the fundamentals of fire fighting, fire prevention, ventilation, local building codes, hazardous materials, first aid, the use and care of equipment, and search and rescue techniques. They learn how to use axes, saws, chemical extinguishers, ladders, and other fire fighting and rescue equipment.

Applicants in some small towns and communities may enter the profession through on-the-job training as volunteer firefighters, or by applying directly to the local government for the position. Once assigned to a fire department, professional firefighters usually serve a probation period ranging from six months to one year. During this time, successful firefighters continue a rigorous training program and are then certified.

Tony remembers his first year as a firefighter in Missoula, Montana, as being extremely difficult and time consuming because of the large amount of material he had to learn. New hires in Missoula are required to become emergency medical technicians, learn every street and block in the 50,000-person city, and demonstrate their ability to correctly handle fire fighting equipment such as hoses and ladders. In addition, they are trained and tested on handling hazardous materials and fighting wildland fires.

LABOR UNIONS

Most career firefighters, especially those in larger cities, are union members. When a person becomes a professional firefighter, he or she has the opportunity to join the International Association of Firefighters. The association was formed in 1918 and strives to promote the welfare of its more than 225,000 members.

Another organization called the International Association of Arson Investigators works to increase the knowledge and skills of professionals who investigate fires, explosions, and related catastrophes.

WHO WILL HIRE ME?

After earning his associate's degree in fire science, Tony tested at ten different departments and made the final list in three cities. He remembers when eleven hundred candidates tested for one position opening up in Olympia, Washington. Although he scored a 96 percent on his written exam, he didn't make the cut.

His family lived in Montana and watched the newspapers for notices of testing periods for fire departments. Tony was visiting his family during one of

Missoula's testing periods, so he decided to try for a position with the Missoula Fire Department. He passed the first section during his visit, and then returned to complete the testing process. Eventually, he was offered a job.

Before he tested in Missoula, Tony had planned to attend a private fire fighting academy to boost his resume—and his chances of getting a job. "I wasn't in a position where I thought I was ready to start testing with departments when I took the test," he remembers. "I still had some things I wanted to do in Southern California in terms of fleshing out my resume. But I thought, 'well, it's kind of hard to turn down a job.' "

Like Tony, most professional firefighters work for a municipal fire department, although some are employed with fire departments on federal and state installations, such as airports, and some serve as wildland firefighters. A small number of professional firefighters work for private companies. Contact these companies directly to inquire about fire fighting positions.

To become a firefighter, you must first test with the hiring department and score high enough to make the "cut" list. Notices of these tests are often listed in newspaper classified advertisements, local job service agencies, or on bulletin boards in public buildings such as post offices and courthouses. The process can prove to be time consuming and expensive. Tony made the cut for the hiring list in Kent, Washington, but he had to travel there four times from Southern California to complete the testing process.

Graduates of two- or four-year fire fighting or fire protection programs can get help from their school placement offices. Applicants may also write or call organizations to inquire about their testing dates and procedures.

Tony also paid to become a member of a subscription service, which forwarded department testing dates as they became available. Several sites on the Internet list testing information, as well as telephone hotlines. "You have to know where to look," he says.

WHERE CAN I GO FROM HERE?

Tony's advancement in the Missoula Fire Department was exceptional. He was hired on as a firefighter at the age of twenty-seven. After a year with the department, a fire inspector position opened up. In Missoula, firefighters need five years under their belt to be eligible to apply for the inspector position, but the city had trouble filling it. So the five-year restriction was dropped, and Tony applied for the position, along with four other candidates.

Now, after serving two years as a fire inspector, Tony is trying to decide which route to take: climb the ladder as a staff member, which means no more fire fighting, or return to the suppression side and eventually try for a job as a captain. That would mean leaving the inspection, public education, and investigation aspects of fire fighting—and taking an initial cut in pay.

Advancement Possibilities

Captains are working supervisors in charge of the technical duties of a fire fighting crew on an engine.

Battalion chiefs oversee captains on major incidents and develop specific strategies to deal with emergency calls.

Fire inspectors work to prevent fires by conducting inspections, public education efforts, and investigations.

Promotional opportunities are good in most fire departments, with firefighters typically advancing at regular intervals for the first three to five years as openings occur. Usually the promotion order is: firefighter, driver/engineer, lieutenant, captain, battalion chief, assistant chief, deputy chief, and chief. Firefighters may work three to five years or more before they are promoted to the position of lieutenant.

Advancement generally depends on scores from written examinations, performance on the job, and seniority, although many departments require formal education, such as an associate's degree, for advancement to the rank of lieutenant, captain, and higher. Fire inspectors in fire departments may become officers or heads of fire prevention bureaus. Fire inspection workers in factories may become plant fire marshals or corporate or plant risk managers. After years of service, some firefighters leave the department or retire and become safety consultants.

WHAT ARE SOME RELATED JOBS?

The U.S. Department of Labor classifies firefighters and fire inspectors under the heading Security Services and Other Protective Service Workers. Also under this heading is the *fire protection engineer,* who identifies fire hazards in homes and workplaces and designs prevention programs and automatic fire detection and extinguishing systems. Other occupations in which workers respond to emergencies include police officers, deputy sheriffs, emergency medical technicians, lifeguards, ski patrollers, park rangers, alarm investigators, corrections officers, detectives, radio dispatchers, security guards, and smoke jumpers.

WHAT ARE THE SALARY RANGES?

Related Jobs

Alarm investigators

Corrections officers

Deputy sheriffs

Detectives

Emergency medical technicians

Fire protection engineers

Lifeguards

Park rangers

Police officers

Radio dispatchers

Security guards

Ski patrollers

Tony started his career as a firefighter making $22,800 a year in 1994. Now, as a fire inspector, he brings in $32,400 annually, which is equivalent to captains' wages in Missoula.

According to the International Association of Firefighters, the average annual salary for firefighters in 1996 was $38,000, but salaries vary widely according to region and the type and size of employer. For example, the average salary for firefighters in the South ranged from $27,800 to $33,600. The same workers in the West earned between $37,200 and $42,400, and between $36,600 and $40,000 in states in the west north central zone, like the Dakotas and Minnesota.

Salaries also vary according to the size of the city, with firefighters in metropolitan areas typically earning more than their counterparts in rural areas. Another salary factor is the number of firefighters working for the establishment. Generally, the higher the number of workers, the higher the pay.

Most fire departments also provide medical and health care coverage, paid sick leave, and pension and retirement benefits, which include disability or service retirement. Service retirement is generally at half-pay after twenty or twenty-five years of service. Vacation periods and personal days are provided, and almost all fire departments furnish appropriate uniforms and safety equipment.

WHAT IS THE JOB OUTLOOK?

Employment of firefighters is expected to increase about as fast as the average for all occupations through the year 2006 because of the nation's steadily increasing population and fire protection needs. The number of paid firefighter positions is expected to increase as a percentage of all firefighter jobs, mainly in smaller but growing communities trying to augment their volunteer force with career firefighters. Little growth is expected in large fire departments located in metropolitan areas.

While buildings are being built with more attention paid to safety, the need for firefighters is not expected to decline. That's because the contents of buildings are still extremely flammable. "It used to be paper and wood and cloth," Tony says. "Now we have polyurethanes and plastics. The building is safer, but what we put in isn't."

Since most people view firefighters as a necessary service, major cuts in fire department funding are not expected. However, given that many local governments are trimming their budgets, Tony wouldn't be surprised if some departments see small funding cuts. He predicts those cuts will likely be restored, though, once a major fire or emergency occurs in the community.

And though he doesn't foresee the need for firefighters declining, Tony does expect professional firefighters to become more specialized, even beyond their current medical calls, hazardous material spills, and rescues. "As things arise in the future, we will meet whatever challenge or danger comes up," he says.

Police Officer

SUMMARY

DEFINITION
Police officers *strive to keep people and property safe by enforcing laws, preserving the peace, preventing criminal acts, investigating crimes, arresting violators, and providing assistance.*

ALTERNATIVE JOB TITLES
Beat officers
Highway patrol officers
Mounted police officer
Patrol officers
State police officers
Traffic police officers

SALARY RANGE
$31,400 to $40,400 to $109,000

EDUCATIONAL REQUIREMENTS
High school diploma

CERTIFICATION OR LICENSING
None

EMPLOYMENT OUTLOOK
As fast as the average

HIGH SCHOOL SUBJECTS
Computer science
Foreign language
Government
Psychology
Sociology

PERSONAL INTERESTS
Exercise/Personal fitness
Helping people: emotionally
Helping people: personal service
Helping people: physical health/medicine
Helping people: protection
Law

Around 2 AM the call comes in: a man and woman are fighting in their home. Police officer Rocky Harris and a senior officer respond. They arrive at the front door of the home, knock on the door, and yell, "Police!" A man comes to the door. "What are you guys doing here?" he snarls. Harris explains that they're concerned that the man and his wife have been fighting, and the officers want to make sure everyone is all right. "Yeah, we've been fighting. What about it?" the man yells. "She's my wife and I can beat her if I want to!"

The officers walk past the man into the house to find his wife. He starts swearing and lunges at them. A fight breaks out, and the man grips Harris' partner's gun and begins to try to remove it from the holster. The officers wrestle him to the floor and handcuff him. They call for backup, arrest the man, and then walk him out to the patrol car. He is still violent and cursing.

Back inside, Harris tries to talk to the man's wife, whose face is swollen and bruised from the beating. The woman is angry with Harris for arresting her husband. After about a half hour of discussing the woman's options, Harris convinces her to get medical treatment for her injuries. After she is transported to the hospital, Harris returns to the police department to begin the booking process on the husband. He is still angry and threatens to kill Officer Harris.

WHAT DOES A POLICE OFFICER DO?

A police officer's duties vary depending on where he or she works. Officers in smaller cities usually perform a wide variety of duties, while officers in larger cities may perform more specialized work, such as identifying firearms, fingerprinting suspects, and investigating criminals. Officers who work for a state government—often known as state troopers or highway patrol officers—spend much of their time patrolling the highways to enforce the laws and regulations.

Police officers in smaller cities—or patrol officers in larger cities—may spend a considerable amount of time patrolling a beat, usually either on foot or in a police car; however, some police departments have turned to more innovative types of beat patrol transportation, including bicycles, horses, and motorcycles. Through their patrols, officers provide a police presence in their community and remain on the lookout for any unusual or suspicious situations. They may also notice stolen cars, missing children, and wanted suspects or criminals. Officers keep in contact with other officers and their headquarters by using two-way radios. They respond to requests for assistance for a variety of reasons including criminal violations, emergency medical situations, rescues, and traffic control. Officers may issue tickets for such things as traffic and parking violations. They may also arrest drunk drivers and respond to domestic dispute calls.

Police officers in larger cities may perform similar duties, or they may work in more specialized units that respond to certain types of calls or incidents. Typically, police departments in large cities are organized into many divisions, each with squads that do special work. Such units include canine divisions, mounted police, and traffic control. Other officers focus their efforts as members of a rescue team or records unit, while some officers work as plainclothes detectives in criminal investigations. In some cities located near large bodies of water, police officers patrol the marinas and watch wharves, docks, and piers for hazards or criminal activities. Harbor patrols may help people or boats in distress, arrest suspects, or help fight fires near the waterway. Other large departments employ helicopter patrols to assist officers with traffic control and disaster assistance. The helicopters are equipped with special spotlights, so they are effective at apprehending suspects fleeing on foot or by car.

Lingo to Learn

Adam codes: *Codes used by some during radio communications to describe types of calls. For example, A1 means arrest, A20 means assistance rendered, and A63 means pursuit.*

Probable cause: *Information developed by an officer to give a reason to arrest, search, or stop and detain a person.*

Reasonable suspicion: *The reasons an officer believes a person should be stopped and detained.*

State police officers usually cruise the highways in patrol cars, monitoring the traffic and driving conditions. They issue traffic tickets or warnings to drivers violating traffic laws, provide assistance for drivers with malfunctioning vehicles, and direct traffic through emergencies or construction zones. State police officers also ensure that drivers and vehicles meet state safety regulations. If an accident occurs, officers may administer first aid to victims, request other emergency personnel, and direct traffic around the site. *Investigative state police officers* work to determine causes of accidents. In addition, some state police departments serve as the primary law enforcement agency for communities that do not have a city or county police force.

"Every day you're assisting the public somehow. You're not out there just busting criminals. A lot of your day is spent just driving around and reacting to things."

Regardless of where they work, most police officers are highly trained in variety of areas, such as firearms use, vehicle pursuit, and self defense. Officers must carry a gun with them on duty, and many officers wear bullet- and knife-resistant vests. All police officers are required to document their work by writing reports—which can involve many hours of paperwork—about their responses to various types of calls. In addition, officers are sometimes called to testify in court about their knowledge of cases with which they have been involved.

WHAT IS IT LIKE TO BE A POLICE OFFICER?

After seventeen years as a police officer at the Missoula Police Department in Montana, thirty-nine-year-old Rocky Harris still likes his job. The satisfaction he gets from helping people has helped him deal with the negative aspects of the job. Harris loves kids, so he enjoys visiting local schools and talking to students about youth violence and gangs. In addition, he likes to teach, so he finds it rewarding to help rookie police officers learn the ropes of the job.

But his primary duty as a police officer is to enforce criminal codes. He's responded to hundreds of calls from the public requesting assistance on everything from lost pets to broken pipes. "Every day you're assisting the public somehow," he says. "You're not out there just busting criminals. A lot of your day is spent just driving around and reacting to things."

And the job varies depending what time of the day it is. During the day, officers often respond to reports of burglaries or vandalism that occurred the night before. At night, officers may find themselves in more potentially dangerous situations dealing with domestic violence, brawls, and rowdy people. "I equate it to being more of a public servant during the day. At night you're doing more arresting," Rocky says.

Police officers in Missoula spend most of their time on routine patrol, with a smaller amount of time spent responding to calls—not necessarily criminal—and writing traffic tickets. And then there are the reports. Officers must write accurate reports on the calls they respond to, and that can take around 20 percent of their time, Rocky says.

Most police departments organize the day into three shifts, with officers rotating through the shifts and generally working at least forty hours a week. Many police officers begin their shift with a briefing from a supervisor on news or information they can use in their work. Officers may work alone, or they may be paired with a partner, and they report back to headquarters at regular intervals, either by radio or computer. Even if a police officer is off duty, he or she is likely to be on call twenty-four hours a day, including weekends and holidays. Officers' varying schedules can be difficult. Rocky often works weekends, nights, and holidays, which interferes with the time he has to spend with his wife and two children.

Police officers may experience stressful and dangerous situations. Officers are responsible for subduing and arresting violent people, including armed robbers and murderers. They try to restore peace and order during riots. They also attempt to rescue or aid victims of automobile accidents, fires, drownings, and more. Many police officers are exposed to death, whether by accident, suicide, or homicide. Officers also must be sure to adhere to local, state, and federal procedures developed for making arrests, searching and seizing property, and upholding citizens' civil rights.

The demanding duties and working conditions of a police officer can be very stressful for the officer, as well as for his or her family. Besides the stress and danger, the physical working conditions may not be pleasant. Police officers respond to calls despite weather conditions, which means they are exposed to blizzards, hurricanes, heat, and other extreme conditions. The work can also be very difficult and tiring, requiring officers to keep in top physical shape. They may be required to engage in a high-speed chase by car, or a strenuous chase on foot. Police officers also must be prepared to defend themselves, or even shoot a person in some cases. Between their bullet-resistant vest and duty belt—which holds tools such as a radio, handcuffs, pepper spray, and their weapon—police officers easily carry twenty pounds of extra weight.

HAVE I GOT WHAT IT TAKES TO BE A POLICE OFFICER?

Most police officers agree that it takes a special kind of person to both enjoy the profession and be successful. High on the list of desirable personal qualifications is honesty, which officers need in order to be trusted with peoples' lives, families, money, and property. Good communication is another key quality, because police officers spend much of their time talking to people of various ethnic backgrounds, cultures, religions, and beliefs.

Rocky says learning to be a good, fair listener is important because police officers often act as mediators and try to resolve conflicts between people. "If I don't solve a problem for someone, I give them ways of solving it for themselves," he says. "Sometimes you have to have the ability to help people realize that they can solve their own problems."

Police officers also must be able to think quickly and make solid decisions, sometimes on the spur of the moment. "Making decisions can have long-term effects on people. A lot of police officers are second-guessed, especially in court," Rocky says, adding that patience and diplomacy are good characteristics for officers to develop.

To be a successful police officer, you should:

Be honest and trustworthy

Have good communication skills

Be patient, fair, and a good listener

Have good physical health, stamina, and agility

Be able to think quickly on your feet and make solid decisions

Enjoy meeting and working with people

And since officers deal with the public on a daily basis, they should enjoy meeting and working with people. "If you don't like people, either you're not going to be a good police officer, or you're going to get out of the job. Because that's what you're doing every day," Rocky says.

Some people may be attracted to the Hollywood version of law enforcement—constant car chases, shootouts, and drama. But there are many routine, unglamorous aspects to the job, so if you're interested in law enforcement solely because of the authority and glory it brings, you may be in for a rude awak-

HAVE I GOT WHAT IT TAKES?, CONTINUED

ening. The actions of police officers are often carefully scrutinized and criticized. If you're in the profession for the wrong reason, the drawbacks to the job will probably overshadow the positive aspects.

Police officers must pass written, physical, and oral tests to measure their intelligence, judgment, and knowledge. They may also be required to pass a vision test, background check, and drug use test. Police officers must be citizens of the United States, they must meet minimum age requirements (usually twenty or twenty-one), and in some cases they must live in the community in which they are seeking employment. Officers also need a driver's license and excellent driving record.

HOW DO I BECOME A POLICE OFFICER?

EDUCATION

High School
Since almost all police departments require applicants to be a high school graduate, plan on it as a necessary requirement. To prepare for a job as police officer, it may help to take classes in psychology, sociology, English, law, mathematics, U.S. government, history, chemistry, physics, foreign languages, and driver education. Computer instruction is becoming more and more important and police departments across the country are using computer technology in a growing number of ways.

One thing high school students can do to prepare themselves for a career in law enforcement, Rocky says, is to get involved with their community and try to improve it. "Know the community that you want to get a job in and understand what the community needs are," he says. "Prepare yourself for the testing process."

Postsecondary Training
While most police departments don't yet require a college degree, the trend is heading in that direction. Several states—including New York, New Jersey, North Dakota, and Iowa—and municipalities require applicants to have a two- or four-year college degree. More and more junior colleges, colleges, and universities are offering programs in law enforcement or administration of justice. While less than 5 percent of police officers in 1970 had a college degree, about a quarter of all police officers today hold a college degree. "Law enforcement is becoming so competitive that soon at least some type of college experience

will be required. At least get a two-year associate's degree, to be competitive," Rocky advises.

After they are hired, most officers in state and large local police departments go through training at a police academy, usually for eight to fourteen weeks. Such training programs are intense and include classroom instruction on topics such as constitutional law and civil rights, state laws and local ordinances, and accident investigation. Recruits may also receive training and supervised experience in patrol, traffic control, weapons and firearms use, self-defense, first aid, safe driving procedures, physical fitness, and emergency response. After the training, new officers usually serve a probationary period lasting from three to six months. In smaller towns, new hires may be trained on the job—rather than at an academy—by working with an experienced officer.

In some states, like Montana, candidates apply directly to the state's law enforcement academy to test for local law enforcement positions. Montana offers regional tests twice a year. Applicants there must pass a written and physical test before they are interviewed by the local hiring department, which then chooses the new officers. Besides academy training, many police departments require new hires to go through a ten- to fourteen-week on-site training program before they become police officers. In addition, police departments require new officers to complete a probationary period.

In Missoula, new hires return from the academy and then spend fourteen weeks in the Field Training Officer (FTO) Program. That's where they learn about police work specifically in Missoula. The program is intense and detailed, requiring the trainees to learn the areas and streets within the city. They are evaluated daily, tested periodically, and can still fail the program— and lose their job with the department.

"What we're doing is gearing the officers toward being able to function as a single officer out in the street, handling calls," Rocky explains. "He's got all the backup in the world out there if he needs it, but he's going to have to function by himself out in the police car." Once a trainee has passed the FTO program, he or she becomes a regular police officer, but still must serve another six months of probation.

INTERNSHIPS AND VOLUNTEERSHIPS

Most police departments have a community outreach program or recruitment program and will visit with interested individuals. Many departments also have a "ride along" program, through which people can ride in a patrol car with a police officer and observe his or her working conditions and duties. High

HOW DO I BECOME A . . . ?, CONTINUED

school graduates may learn more about the life of a police officer by becoming a police cadet in a large city police department. Cadets are paid employees who work part-time performing clerical or other duties for a police department. They may be allowed to attend training courses, and then apply to become a regular police officer once they are old enough. In addition, some police departments hire college students as interns.

LABOR UNIONS

Many police officers who work for cities belong to the city's bargaining unit, which negotiates city employees' salaries and benefits. In addition, some police officers belong to the National Fraternal Order of Police, or the International Union of Police Associations (AFL-CIO).

Rocky is required to be a member of the Missoula Police Protective Association, which negotiates police officers' contracts in Missoula.

WHO WILL HIRE ME?

Rocky was a college student at the University of Montana, studying to be a math and science teacher, when he became interested in law enforcement—quite by accident. While working as a bartender to help pay his college costs, Rocky met and became friendly with the police officers who walked the beat where he worked. He talked to them about their jobs and thought the job of a police officer might be something he would enjoy. He went on several "ride-alongs" with officers to learn more about their duties and work environment. Then he started playing on the police officers' softball team and got to know the officers—and their way of life. When an opening came along, several officers encouraged Rocky to apply. He did, and eventually got the job. "It's not something that I had wanted to do all my life," he says.

Most police officers work for local governments, with some finding employment with a state department, and a small percentage working for a federal agency. The U.S. has more than 18,000 municipal police agencies, 3,000 county sheriff departments, and 1,200 state and federal police agencies. In the early 1990s, local police departments employed about 604,000 full-time sworn police officers with general arrest powers. Large cities each employ thousands of police officers. In 1997, New York had 31,000 police officers, and Chicago employed nearly 13,000 police officers.

Local civil service rules and state laws govern the hiring of police officers in almost all large cities and most small cities. Contact the department directly to find out where to apply for a position. Some cities offer a local civil service office or examining board. In small cities, candidates usually apply directly to the department. If you are interested in working for a state or federal government, contact the agency to inquire about the application process.

Check law enforcement trade journals for advertisements. The Internet offers many law enforcement employment sites, as well as the Web sites of specific law enforcement agencies. Local job service agencies and newspapers also advertise police officer positions.

Police officers may also find employment working at a college or university. Others work for private companies providing security or investigative services.

WHERE CAN I GO FROM HERE?

Rocky worked for six and a half years as a patrol officer after he was hired in 1981. Then he applied for a lateral position in the department's detective division. He then spent eight years—five years in narcotics and three years in juvenile crime—before moving back out to the uniform patrol division. He specifically left the detective's division because he thought a sergeant's position was going to open up in the patrol division. He was right. The sergeant's position became available, and Rocky tested for the job and got it.

Now, after eighteen months as a sergeant, Rocky says he'll apply and test for the next lieutenant's position that becomes available. Eventually he may apply for a captain's position, which is appointed by the department's chief. In 2001, when he is forty-three years old, Rocky will have the option to retire and receive a pension of half his pay. The longer he stays past his twenty years of service, the more his pension will be. He's got about one year left of college to become qualified to teach math and science, and he may consider doing just that in a few years. "I'm not going to leave this job just because I'm able to," he says.

In general, advancement is determined by length of service, job performance, formal education and training courses, and test scores. Depending on the department, promotions usually become available six months to three years after hiring. The progression of pro-

Advancement Possibilities

Sergeants *are first-line supervisors that work directly with the police officers. They evaluate and train officers, make assignments, and schedule shifts.*

Lieutenants *are mid-level managers that occasionally work the streets. They concentrate more on personnel issues and the management of patrol teams.*

Captains *oversee a major unit within a department and develop a budget and approve expenditures. In some departments this is an appointed position.*

WHERE CAN I GO FROM HERE?, CONTINUED

motion is typically police officer, detective, sergeant, lieutenant, captain, assistant chief, and chief, depending on the department's structure. Larger departments usually have additional top-level management positions, such as division, bureau, or department directors. These positions, and that of chief, are often made by direct political appointment.

WHAT ARE SOME RELATED JOBS?

The U.S. Department of Labor classifies police officers under the heading Investigating Occupations and Police Officers and Detectives, Public Service. Some related jobs include FBI special agents, immigration officers, customs officials, border patrol officers, U.S. marshals, state highway patrol officers, sheriffs, deputy sheriffs, detectives, correctional officers, fire wardens, firefighters and inspectors, special agents, security officers, military police, and private investigators, wildlife agents, and fish and game wardens.

Big city police departments—and some other law enforcement agencies—need other workers to perform administrative and record-keeping duties. These big agencies also hire people to work in more specialized fields, such as forensics. In addition, some agencies hire civilian employees to work in their traffic accident division, which responds to and investigates accidents.

Related Jobs

Border patrol officers

Correctional officers

Customs officials

Deputy sheriffs

Detectives

FBI special agents

Fire fighters and inspectors

Fire wardens

Fish and game wardens

Immigration officers

Military police

Private investigators

Security officers

Sheriffs

Special agents

State highway patrol officers

U.S. marshals

Wildlife agents

WHAT ARE THE SALARY RANGES?

Missoula pays its starting police officers a salary of about $24,000 a year, with the high-end of patrol officer pay reaching about $30,000 a year. As a sergeant, Rocky now makes $38,000 a year, and that will likely increase before the new year, as will the lieutenant's salary of $42,000 a year.

Nationwide, larger departments typically offer slightly higher pay for police officers. Regionally, western states generally pay better, and southern states often pay lower salaries. According to the Police Labor Monthly Salary

Tracker, the average minimum salary for police officers in the United States in 1997 was $31,400. That figure dropped to an average of $25,800 in the South and jumped to an average of $35,100 in the West. After ten years of service, the average salary for police officers was $40,400, ranging from $34,000 in the South to $45,300 in the West.

For assistant police chiefs, the average minimum salary in 1997 ranged from $58,700 in the west north central to $78,000 in the Northeast. The average maximum salary for assistant police chiefs ranged from $66,700 in the South to $99,500 in the West. For police chiefs, the average minimum salary ranged from $63,600 in the west north central to $87,400 in the Northeast. The average maximum salary for chiefs ranged from $83,000 in the west north central to $109,000 in the West.

In Missoula—and most police agencies across the country—police officers' benefits include vacation and sick leave, medical insurance, compensatory time/holiday pay, retirement, deferred compensation, tuition reimbursement, and overtime, which is common and can be significant. Most police departments provide uniforms, weapons, handcuffs, and other required equipment.

WHAT IS THE JOB OUTLOOK?

With the increase in violent crimes committed by young people, law enforcement has become a more prevalent issue among many Americans. At the same time, budget cuts experienced by many municipalities have put a limit on the resources available for local police departments. Only time will tell how these two opposing forces will find a balance. For now, the employment of police officers is expected to increase about as fast as the average.

In the meantime, many communities are seeing a push toward community policing—building partnerships with the citizens of neighborhoods to increase the public's confidence in police, and mobilize the public to help police officers fight crime. With community policing, officers encourage citizens to take an active role in crime prevention and response. Some police officers have moved their homes to higher-crime neighborhoods in an effort to become a more permanent, higher profile figure in the neighborhood and community.

The salaries and benefits of police officers are viewed as attractive by many and the number of qualified candidates is expected to continue to exceed the number of available positions. As a result, the field is becoming

WHAT IS THE JOB OUTLOOK?, CONTINUED

more and more competitive, with applicants bringing more substantial resumes to the screening process. Candidates with college training will likely prove to be more competitive than those with high school diplomas, although relevant experience also can help.

Opportunities for police officers are expected to be better in urban communities where crime is somewhat higher, and officers' pay is relatively low. Departments in these areas are having trouble recruiting high quality police officer candidates.

Rocky says police work changes with society. "When I started work here I never thought I'd be going to high school criminology classes and talking about gangs or talking about the number of drugs out on the streets," he says. "The basis of crime is always going to be there, it's just going to get more sophisticated, so law enforcement needs to get more sophisticated."

And it is. Departments are using computers in new ways to help streamline their operations. The Internet has also provided a new source of information to departments and allows them to learn more from their peers across the country.

Crime Stats

A 1997 survey conducted by Global Strategy Group Inc. for the National Association of Police Organizations found:

Most people believe law enforcement agencies should concentrate on fighting drug use and trafficking, violent crimes, gang violence, child abuse, and keeping the peace.

70 percent of people think police officers in the United States are underpaid.

42 percent of people worry about becoming a victim of a crime, while 44 percent say they or someone in their family have been a victim of a crime.

94 percent of people think states should be required to conduct a background check on individuals trying to purchase guns.

80 percent of people think additional funding should be provided for juvenile prevention programs.

76 percent of people think the drug problem in America has gotten worse.

Secret Service Special Agent

SUMMARY

DEFINITION
U.S. Secret Service Special Agents work to protect the president and other political leaders of the United States, as well as heads of foreign states or governments when they are visiting the United States. Special agents also investigate financial crimes and work to suppress the counterfeiting of U.S. currency.

ALTERNATIVE JOB TITLES
None

SALARY RANGE
$31,550 to $66,825 to $115,700

EDUCATIONAL REQUIREMENTS
Bachelor's degree

CERTIFICATION OR LICENSING
None

EMPLOYMENT OUTLOOK
About as fast as the average

HIGH SCHOOL SUBJECTS
Computer science
English (writing/literature)
Foreign language
Government
Physical education
Psychology

PERSONAL INTERESTS
Computers
Current events
Exercise/Personal fitness
Helping people: protection
Law
Travel

Bands play and crowds cheer as President Clinton strides from Air Force One to a waiting armored limousine at the Pittsburgh Airport. Once he is safely in the car, the motorcade begins driving to the site of a convention where the president will speak.

Secret Service special agent Norm Jarvis is riding in the car behind Clinton's limo. It's quiet inside the car, except for the occasional crackle of the radio, alerting the agents to potential problems. Jarvis and the other agents look intently out the windows at the streets lined with people hoping to catch a glimpse of the president. "There's a group of protesters ahead on the left," he tells his co-workers. On the right side of the road he sees a group of waving school children holding a banner that reads, "Stop here, Mr. President!"

Things are quiet for the next few minutes. Then suddenly Jarvis hears a loud "Bang! Bang!" His heart jumps for a second before he realizes the sound is not gunfire but merely a backfire from one of the police motorcycles driving alongside the car. He breathes deeply for a moment, then focuses his mind back on the job at hand—protecting the president of the United States.

WHAT DOES A SPECIAL AGENT DO?

The U.S. Secret Service employs about four thousand six hundred people, two thousand of whom are special agents. Secret Service special agents are charged with two missions: protecting U.S. leaders or visiting foreign dignitaries, and investigating the counterfeiting of U.S. currency. Special agents are empowered to carry and use firearms, execute warrants, and make arrests.

Besides the president, vice president, and their immediate families, special agents work to ensure the safety of a number of other individuals (see sidebar). Special agents work continually to protect certain U.S. leaders, like the president, and when a government summit is held in the United States or abroad, special agents are responsible for protecting either the visiting foreign leaders, or the American leaders who have traveled to a foreign country.

Lingo to Learn

Choke point: *A potential ambush site—like a bridge—where a protectee or motorcade may be more vulnerable to attack.*

Protective bubble: *A 360-degree virtual boundary of safety that the Secret Service maintains around each of its protectees. Special agents work to ensure that nothing dangerous penetrates the bubble.*

Protectee: *A person—usually a political leader of the United States or a foreign dignitary—that the Secret Service is responsible for protecting. Protectees may also include the spouse or family of the primary protectee.*

When assigned to a permanent protection duty—for the president, for example—special agents are usually assigned to the Washington, DC area. They are responsible for planning and executing protective operations for their protectee at all times. Agents can also be assigned to a temporary protective duty to provide protection for candidates or visiting foreign dignitaries. In either case, an advance team of special agents surveys each site that will be visited by the protectee. Based on their survey, the team determines how much manpower and what types of equipment are needed to provide protection. They identify hospitals and evacuation routes, and work closely with local police, fire, and rescue units to develop the protection plan and determine emergency routes and procedures, should the need arise. Then a command post is set up with secure communications to act as the communication center for protective activities. The post monitors emergencies and keeps participants in contact with each other.

Before the protectees arrive, the *lead advance agent* coordinates all law enforcement representatives participating in the visit. The assistance of military, federal, state, county, and local law enforcement organizations is a vital part of the entire security operation. Personnel are told where they will be posted and are alerted to specific problems associated with the visit. Intelligence information is discussed and emergency measures are outlined. Just prior to the arrival of the protectee, checkpoints are established and access to the secure area is limited. After the visit, special agents analyze every step of the protective operation, record unusual incidents, and suggest improvements for future operations.

Protective research is an important part of all security operations. *Protective research engineers* and *protective research technicians* develop, test, and maintain technical devices and equipment needed to provide a safe environment for the protectee.

When assigned to an investigative duty, special agents investigate threats against Secret Service protectees. They also work to detect and arrest people committing any offense relating to coins, currency, stamps, government bonds, checks, credit card fraud, computer fraud, false identification crimes, and other obligations or securities of the United States. Special agents also investigate violations of the Federal Deposit Insurance Act, the Federal Land Bank Act, and the Government Losses in Shipment Act. Special agents assigned to an investigative duty usually work in one of the Secret Service's 125 domestic and foreign field offices. Agents assigned to investigative duties in a field office are often called out to serve on a temporary protective operation.

Special agents assigned to investigate financial crimes may also be assigned to one of the Secret Service's three divisions in Washington, DC, or they may receive help from the divisions while conducting an investigation from a field office. The Counterfeit Division constantly reviews the latest reprographic and lithographic technologies to keep a step ahead of counterfeiters. The Financial Crimes Division aids special agents in their investigation of electronic crimes involving credit cards, computers, cellular and regular telephones, narcotics, illegal firearms trafficking, homicide, and other crimes. The Forensic Services Division coordinates forensic science activities within the Secret Service. The division analyzes evidence such as documents, fingerprints, photographs, and video and audio recordings.

The Secret Service employs a number of specialist positions such as electronics engineers, communications technicians, research psychologists, computer experts, armorers, intelligence analysts, polygraph examiners, forensic experts, security specialists, and more.

WHAT IS IT LIKE TO BE A SPECIAL AGENT?

For more than thirteen years, Norm Jarvis has been a special agent for the Secret Service. He has protected a variety of U.S. political leaders including President Bill Clinton and past presidents Nixon, Carter, and Ford. He has also protected foreign dignitaries including the president of Sudan and the prime minister of Israel. In addition, Norm has investigated criminal activity in a number of cities and is now serving as the field officer of the Secret Service's Montana office.

While his primary responsibility is to investigate crimes, Norm is called out regularly to protect a political or foreign leader. During those times, the forty-three-year-old serves as a member of a team of special agents who work to ensure there is always a "protective bubble" surrounding the protectee, regardless of whether he or she is in a moving or stationary location. Protective operations can be complicated, with special agents working together around the clock, using intelligence and special technologies, and working in conjunction with local authorities to make sure the protectee is safe. "We don't believe anybody can do bodyguard work just by walking around with somebody," Norm says. "Scowls and large muscles don't mean a lot if somebody is bound and determined to kill you." While special agents don't change their protective techniques when they work overseas, they often work in conjunction with foreign security agencies. "Other security forces usually defer to the Secret Service, which is considered a premier security agency," Norm says.

When Norm is not on a protective assignment, he spends his time investigating a variety of crimes. Special agents assigned to smaller field offices typically handle a wide variety of criminal investigations. But special agents usually work for a specialized squad in a field office, handling specific investigations like counterfeit currency, forgery, and financial crimes. Special agents may receive case referrals from the Secret Service headquarters, other law enforcement agencies, or through their own investigations. Investigating counterfeit money requires extensive undercover operations and surveillance. Special agents usually work with the U.S. Attorney's Office and local law enforcement for counterfeit cases. Through their work, special agents detect and seize millions of dollars of coun-

The Secret Service: Yesterday and Today

The Secret Service was established in 1865 to suppress the counterfeiting of U.S. currency. After the assassination of President William McKinley in 1901, the Secret Service was directed by Congress to protect the president of the United States.

Today, it is the Secret Service's responsibility to protect:

The president, vice president, and their immediate families.

Former presidents and their spouses for their lifetimes. (Spousal protection will terminate if they remarry.)

Children of former presidents until they are sixteen years old.

Visiting heads of foreign states or governments and their spouses traveling with them, along with other distinguished foreign visitors to the United States.

Official representatives of the United States who are performing special missions abroad.

Major presidential and vice presidential candidates, and within 120 days of the general presidential election, their spouses.

terfeit money each year—some of which is produced overseas. Special agents working in a fraud squad often receive complaints or referrals from banking or financial institutions that have been defrauded. Fraud investigations involve painstaking and long-term investigations to reveal the criminals, who are usually organized groups or individuals hiding behind false identifications. Special agents working for forgery squads are often referred to cases from banks or local police departments that have discovered incidents of forgery.

"It's important as a representative of the President's Office that you conduct yourself well . . . and that you're able to command some respect."

Protective and investigative assignments can keep a special agent away from home for long periods of time, depending on the situation. Preparations for the president's visits to cities in the United States generally take no more than a week. But a large event attracting foreign dignitaries—the Asian Pacific Conference in the state of Washington, for example—can take months to plan. Special agents are already working on providing a safe environment for the 2002 Winter Olympics to be held in Salt Lake City. That's because of the sheer size and large numbers of people who will attend. Special agents at field offices assigned to investigate crimes are called out regularly to serve temporary protective missions. During campaign years, agents typically serve three-week protective assignments, work three weeks back at their field office, and then start the process over again. Special agents always work at least forty hours a week and often work a minimum of fifty hours each week.

HAVE I GOT WHAT IT TAKES TO BE A SPECIAL AGENT?

The Secret Service is looking for smart, upstanding citizens who will favorably represent the U.S. government. The agency looks for people with strong ethics, morals, and virtues—and then they teach them how to be a special agent. "You can be a crackerjack lawyer, but have some ethical problems in your background, and we wouldn't hire you as an agent even though we would love to have your expertise," Norm says.

Special agents also need dedication, which can be demonstrated through a candidate's grade point average in high school and college. And applicants must have a drug-free background. Even experimental drug use can be a reason to dismiss an applicant from the hiring process. Special agents also need to be confident and honest—with no criminal background. "It's important as a representative of the President's Office that you conduct yourself well, that you look good, and that you're able to command some respect," Norm says. "Anything even as minor as shoplifting is an indicator of a personality problem."

Since special agents must travel for their jobs—Norm spends about 30 percent of his time on the road—interested applicants should be flexible and willing to be away from home. Norm says the traveling is one of the downfalls of the job, often requiring him to leave his wife and two children with a moment's notice.

To be a successful Secret Service special agent, you should:

Have strong ethics, morals, and virtues

Be confident and honest, with no criminal background

Be flexible and willing to work away from home at a moment's notice

Be highly intelligent and able to act quickly in an emergency

Be willing to risk injury or loss of life in the course of your protective duties

One of the drawbacks of being a special agent is the potential danger involved. A special agent was shot in the stomach in 1981 during an assassination attempt on President Ronald Reagan. Other agents have been killed on the job in helicopter accidents, surveillance assignments, and protective operations, to name a few.

But the benefits outweigh the drawbacks for most agents. For Norm, the excitement and profound importance of his work gives him great job satisfaction. "There are times when you are involved in world history and you witness history being made, or you are present when historical decisions are being made, and you feel privileged to be a part of making history, albeit you're behind the scenes and never recognized for it," he says, noting he finds the job fascinating. However, the job is not always glamorous, and can be "like going out in your backyard in your best suit and standing for three hours," according to one of Norm's co-workers.

HOW DO I BECOME A SPECIAL AGENT?

EDUCATION

High School

You can help prepare for a career as a special agent by doing well in high school. You may receive special consideration by the Secret Service if you have computer training, which is needed to investigate computer fraud, or if you can speak a foreign language, which is useful during investigations and while protecting visiting heads of state or U.S. officials who are working abroad. Specialized skills are highly regarded in electronics, forensics, and other investigative areas. Aside from school, doing something unique and positive for your city or neighborhood, or becoming involved in community organizations can improve your chances of being selected by the Secret Service.

The Secret Service also offers the Stay-In-School Program for high school students. The program allows students who meet financial eligibility guidelines to earn money and some benefits by working part-time, usually in a clerical job for the agency. There are many requirements and application guidelines for this program, so contact the Secret Service's Stay-In-School office at 202-435-5800.

Postsecondary Training

The Secret Service recruits special agents at the GS-5 and GS-7 grade levels. You can qualify at the GS-5 level in one of three ways: obtain a four-year degree from an accredited college or university; work for at least three years in a criminal investigative or law enforcement field, and gain knowledge and experience in applying laws relating to criminal violations; or obtain an equivalent combination of education and experience. You can qualify at the GS-7 level by achieving superior academic scores (defined as a grade point average of at least 2.95 on a 4.0 scale), going to graduate school and studying a directly related field, or gaining an additional year of criminal investigative experience.

All newly hired special agents go through nine weeks of training at the Federal Law Enforcement Training Center in Glynco, Georgia, and then eleven weeks of specialized training at the Secret Service's Training Academy in Beltsville, Maryland. During training, new agents take comprehensive courses in protective techniques, criminal and constitutional law, criminal investigative procedures, use of scientific investigative devices, first aid, the use of firearms, and defensive measures. Special agents also learn about collecting evidence, surveillance techniques, undercover operation, and courtroom demeanor. Specialized training includes skills such as fire fighting and protection aboard airplanes. The classroom study is supplemented by on-the-job training, and special agents go through advanced in-service training throughout their careers.

New special agents usually begin work at the field office where they first applied. Their initial work is investigative in nature and is closely supervised. After around five years, agents are usually transferred to a protection assignment.

INTERNSHIPS AND VOLUNTEERSHIPS

The Secret Service offers the Cooperative Education Program as a way for the agency to identify and train highly motivated students for a career as a special agent. Participants of the paid program learn more about the Secret Service and gain on-the-job training, with the possibility of working full-time for the Secret Service upon graduation. The two-year work-study program includes classroom training and hands-on training that will prepare students for the following Secret Service careers: accountant, budget analyst, computer specialist, computer research specialist, electronic engineer, intelligence research specialist, management specialist, personnel management specialist, telecommunications specialist, and visual information specialist. Students working towards a bachelor's degree must complete one thousand and forty hours of study-related work requirements.

To be considered for the program, you must: be enrolled full-time in an accredited educational program; be enrolled in your school's cooperative education program; maintain a 3.0 grade point average in either undergraduate or graduate studies; be a U.S. citizen; be enrolled in a field of study related to the position you are applying for; pass a drug test; and pass a preliminary background investigation and possibly a polygraph test.

Students in the program work part-time, which is between sixteen and thirty-two hours a week. They may work full-time during holidays and school breaks. They receive some federal benefits including a pension plan, low-cost life and health insurance, annual and sick leave, holiday pay, awards, and promotions.

You must submit a variety of forms to apply for this program, so contact the Secret Service's Co-Op coordinator at 202-435-5800 for more information. In addition, you may be able to apply for the program through the cooperative education program at your school.

WHO WILL HIRE ME?

Norm didn't set out to become a special agent. As a teenager, he admired a neighbor who worked as a deputy sheriff. As Norm grew older and had to make decisions about college and work, he realized he wanted to go into law enforcement. At the age of eighteen, he volunteered to go into the U.S. Army to train with the military police. When Norm left the service, he used his VA benefits to help him get a bachelor's degree in psychology from Westminster College. "I have an innate interest in why people do the things they do," he says. Norm also earned a master's degree in public administration from Utah University. He spent eight years working as a police officer before he decided to apply with the Secret Service. He wasn't satisfied with his police officer's salary and was tired of the "day-to-day emotional trauma of being an officer." Norm loved to travel and was impressed by some special agents he had met, so he decided that becoming a special agent would be a way for him to progress professionally and work in an exciting position. He applied for the job and began working as a special agent assigned to Salt Lake City in 1984.

The Secret Service warns that because they have many well-qualified applicants and few anticipated vacancies, the likelihood that you will get hired is limited. On top of that, the hiring process can take up to a year—or longer—because of the thoroughness of the selection process. All special agent candidates must pass a thorough personal interview, the Treasury Enforcement Agent Examination, a physical examination, a polygraph test, drug screening, and an extensive background investigation. The most qualified candidates will then go through in-depth interviews.

The successful applicant must be in excellent physical condition, with weight proportionate to his or her height. Candidates' distant vision must be at least 20/60 in each eye uncorrected, and 20/20 in each eye corrected; their near vision must be at least 20/40 corrected. Newly appointed special agents must be at least twenty-one years old and less than thirty-seven years old when they are appointed, and they must be U.S. citizens. They may be assigned to work anywhere in the United States, and throughout their careers agents will travel frequently and be reassigned periodically to Secret Service offices in the United States or a foreign liaison assignment in a different country.

If you can make it through the tough screening process and get hired, you'll be employed by the U.S. Secret Service, which is part of the Department of the Treasury. If you're ready to apply for a special agent job, make sure you meet the requirements described above. Then submit a typewritten Standard Form 171, Application for Federal Employment. If you went to college, you will also need to submit an official transcript. Alternatively, you can submit an

Optional Application for Federal Employment or a resume, but you'll have to complete some accompanying forms, so be sure to check with the Secret Service field office nearest you before doing so to find out exactly what forms to fill out. The field office in your area should be listed in the government section of your telephone book.

To find out what vacancies currently exist with the Secret Service, call their personnel division at 202-435-5800.

WHERE CAN I GO FROM HERE?

Norm began working in the Secret Service's Salt Lake City field office in 1984. He was transferred to the Organized Crime Task Force in the Washington, DC field office in 1987. In 1990 Norm was promoted to the position of instructor at the Office of Training, and he was transferred to the Presidential Protective Division in 1994. Norm ended up in Montana in 1997 after being promoted to the position of resident agent of the Great Falls field office.

Advancement Possibilities

Assistants to the special agent in charge supervise a squad of agents in a field office.

Special agents in charge oversee a field office or protective detail.

Deputy assistant directors help manage the Secret Service's headquarters, field offices, and protective details.

Generally, special agents begin their career by spending seven to ten years performing primarily investigative duties at a field office. Then they are usually assigned to a protective assignment for three to five years. After twelve or thirteen years, special agents become eligible to move into a supervisory position. A typical promotion path moves special agents to the position of senior agent, then resident agent in charge of a district, assistant to the special agent in charge, and finally special agent in charge of a field office or headquarters division. Since the Secret Service employs many highly skilled professionals, promotions are very competitive and are awarded based upon performance.

Special agents can retire after they have twenty years of work under their belt, and after they are fifty years old. Special agents must retire before the age of fifty-seven. Although Norm can retire in six years, he's enjoying his job and plans to continue working with the Secret Service. "I plan on learning a lot about Montana, its people, and this area of the world," he says. "I always thought about the future and what I wanted to do. Now the future is here." When he does retire, Norm does not plan on pursuing law enforcement activities. Instead, he'd like to earn a doctorate in psychology, sociology, or criminology and teach at the college level.

Other retired agents get hired to organize logistics for corporations needing to get either people or products from one place to another. Other agents work as bodyguards, private investigators, security consultants, and local law enforcement officials.

WHAT ARE SOME RELATED JOBS?

The U.S. Department of Labor classifies special agents under the heading Investigating Occupations. Also under this heading are private investigators, fire wardens, FBI agents, customs patrol officers, deputy sheriffs, U.S. marshals, detectives, fish and game wardens, narcotics investigators, police officers, state highway patrol officers, and regional wildlife agents. Special agents are also classified with public service police officers, border guards, and fingerprint classifiers.

Related Jobs

Border guards
Customs patrol officers
Deputy sheriffs
Detectives
FBI agents
Fingerprint classifiers
Fire wardens
Fish and game wardens
Narcotics investigators
Police officers
Private investigators
Public service police officers
Regional wildlife agents
State highway patrol officers
U.S. marshals

Besides employing special agents, the Secret Service hires uniformed division officers and various professional, administrative, technical, and clerical workers. Most positions other than those of special agent are located in the Washington, DC area. Uniformed division officers are responsible for protecting the White House Complex, other governmental offices, the president and his immediate family, and the vice president's home and family. Among a lengthy list of other requirements, uniformed division officer applicants must be at least twenty-one years old and have a high school diploma.

WHAT ARE THE SALARY RANGES?

Special agents generally receive law enforcement availability pay on top of their base pay. Agents usually start at the GS-5 or GS-7 grade levels, which were $31,550 and $35,900 in 1997, respectively, including the availability pay. (Salaries may be slightly higher in some areas with high costs of living.) Agents automatically advance by two pay grades each year, until they reach the GS-12 level, which was $56,190 in 1997. Agents must compete for positions above the

WHAT ARE THE SALARY RANGES?, CONTINUED

GS-12 level; however, the majority of agents become a GS-13—$66,825 in 1997—in their career. Top officials in the Secret Service are appointed to Senior Executive Service (SES) positions who do not receive the availability pay. The top SES salary in 1997 was $115,700.

Benefits for special agents include low-cost health and life insurance; annual and sick leave; paid holidays; a comprehensive retirement program. In addition, free financial protection is provided to agents and their families in the event of job-related injury or death.

WHAT IS THE JOB OUTLOOK?

Compared to other federal law enforcement agencies, the Secret Service is small. The agency focuses on its protective missions and isn't interested in expanding its responsibilities. "We want to be the best at protection, and I think we are the best in the world and that suits us fine," Norm says. As a result, the Secret Service will likely not grow much, unless the president and Congress decide to expand the agency's duties.

Since the Secret Service employs a small number of people, their new hires each year are limited. The agency anticipates hiring another roughly one hundred special agents in 1998. Officials anticipate the job availability will remain about the same, although it could increase slightly over the next few years.

What Can I Do Right Now?

public safety

Get Involved

If you've made it this far through the book, it's probably because a career in public safety is starting to sound like a definite possibility. You're committed to serving your community and, even after reading the career profiles, you aren't discouraged by the dangers and difficulties experienced by virtually everyone in this field. Chances are that if you're this interested in working for the public safety now, you'd rather not wait until high school graduation to start working toward your chosen career. The good news—which you may have guessed from the title of the book—is that you don't have to.

It's true that there aren't as many established ways for teenagers to prepare for public safety careers as there are to prepare for careers in, say, the environment. In that field, there are any number of universities offering pre-college courses for high school students and state parks, animal sanctuaries, and activist groups offering internship and employment opportunities. You're unlikely to find many comparable opportunities in public safety, mainly because of state and local regulations on the age and amount of training required for those working in the field.

This may seem a trifle unfair, especially if your community has particularly strict regulations. But lives and the safety of people and property are on the line in this industry and they must be safeguarded by every possible means. You surely know from personal experience that some people under the age of eighteen—or even twenty-one—are just not mature or responsible enough to work in public safety. On the other hand, some young people *do* have the capability and commitment to start actively pursuing careers from fire fighting to the Secret Service. And if you are one of those people, there *are* things you can do right now.

Preparing for a career in public safety can entail a fairly broad range of activities, many of which are listed in this section. The ones you choose will depend upon how certain you are of your career choice, how much time you can and will devote now to career preparation, and which options are available or practicable in your community. Some activities are directly linked to specific careers, to the point where you are effectively a police cadet or junior firefighter. Others involve you with people working in the field or expose you to the work they do. Still other activities help you acquire the kinds of skills and characteristics needed in public safety jobs. We don't endorse any particular organizations or activities, but we do encourage you to research and explore them for yourself.

THE DIRECT ROUTE TO PUBLIC SAFETY CAREERS

If you think you're ready to make a serious career commitment—or at the very least a serious time commitment—then this is the section for you. Many of the programs here demand several hours of your free time, meaning the time you now spend on studying, socializing, working at a paying job, or pursuing other extracurricular activities. Some are connected to your high school curriculum, others are concerned with your college career—including your summer breaks and post-graduation plans.

These kinds of commitments are always a bit intimidating, but the rewards they bring can be amazing. If you're interested in an intelligence career, some of the programs listed here can guarantee an intelligence job waiting for you as soon as you complete your college degree. If you're pursuing a vo-tech program in law enforcement now, joining the VICA organization as explained here can lead you toward national recognition in your field. If you want to be a firefighter, the Explorers program can have you working in a fire station before you even finish high school.

If you're serious about a career in public safety, these programs are serious about helping you make it happen.

BSA EXPLORERS

BSA stands for Boy Scouts of America, but if you're a woman, don't let that stop you from reading this section! The BSA Explorers program is for everybody—it just happens to have been started by the Boy Scouts. They believe, as you do, that when hands-on career experience is available to people still in their teens, it makes them especially well prepared to enter the world of work after graduation from high school or college. So they've developed the Explorers program for young people between the ages of fourteen and twenty. Groups of young people—sometimes from established Boy Scout troops, sometimes not—with a common interest in a specific career form their own Explorer posts to pursue that interest. And what are some of the most popular careers for exploration? Law enforcement, fire fighting, and emergency medical services.

Explorer posts in these career areas are actually part of their communities' regular public safety services. For example, law enforcement Explorer posts are part of their cities' or townships' police departments. Student members of the posts are guided by adult leaders (i.e., an actual police officer or firefighter), but are themselves responsible for planning activities and ensuring that the post functions as it should. Democracy is the guiding principle of each Explorer post, and activities are carried out in a completely voluntary, supportive, and adventurous environment.

All Explorers must subscribe to a code of convictions and duties and, as part of their post, work on goals and activities addressing career, leadership, fitness, social, service, and outdoor concerns. Each post also establishes membership and organization rules and a code of conduct designed to protect both the Explorers and the community they serve. Young people must live up to their responsibilities in the Explorer post or face not attaining or losing full membership.

Emergency Medical Services Explorers

Explorer posts with this specialty can be quite difficult to locate, largely due to the huge responsibilities of EMS and the medical training needed to undertake them. There are also logistical problems: administering medications may be age-restricted, driving the ambulance is generally not for teenagers, and rescue squads often have no room for anyone but the patient and one or two EMTs.

Despite all this, some Explorer posts are still able to specialize in emergency medical services. Explorers in these posts help the EMTs maintain their medical equipment and keep the ambulance in a state of readiness. They may ride to emergency situations in a special car ahead of or behind the rescue squad and perform basic support tasks at the scene. Explorers sometimes help out when the EMS runs blood pressure checks or cholesterol screenings for the community.

You'll need to get in touch with your community's own emergency medical services (possibly affiliated with the fire department) to see if they have an Explorer post or are interested in setting up one.

Fire Fighting Explorers

Although many states and cities bar young people from actually fighting fires, those who are members of Explorer posts are able to help their local fire departments maintain their equipment, assist in drills, and perform support tasks when a fire is being fought. Again depending on local rules and regulations, some Explorers are able to fight small brush fires, which do not threaten lives or property.

Naturally, personal safety has to be a top priority for firefighters and you're sure to learn safety techniques and precautionary measures from working with the professionals, even if you never get to fight a single fire while in the Explorers. You'll also gain an understanding and appreciation of teamwork when you witness and experience the trust firefighters put in each other.

Your community's fire department can tell you if they're at all involved with Explorers.

Law Enforcement Explorers

Law enforcement is an exceedingly popular Explorer post specialty endorsed by such organizations as the International Association of Chiefs of Police and the National Sheriff's Association. Fortunately, there are more than 2,800 law enforcement Explorer posts around the country, so you just might find one in your area.

Explorers in these posts assist police officers in such matters as crime prevention, traffic control, and facilitating community events. Some Explorers participate in the Ride-Along Program, which entails accompanying police officers on their patrols. These Explorers experience the job first-hand and assist their officers when someone in the community calls for help. Special care is taken not to involve students riding-along in dangerous situations such as shoot-outs.

It is important to remember that, although Explorers take on important policing responsibilities, work with police officers, and wear modified police uniforms, they are *not* police officers. They must never pretend to be (that's impersonating a police officer, and it's a crime!) and they must never place themselves in a situation where a trained professional is required.

Contact your local police department if you are interested in joining or setting up a law enforcement Explorer post.

Starting Your Own Explorer Post

As we've said, the simplest and most direct way to get involved with the Explorers program is to contact your local police, fire, or EMS department and see if there is already an Explorer post for you to join. Very often, however, there won't be one. Don't let that discourage you from getting involved; it's really just an opportunity to start your own post and take a leadership role in running it.

If, when you contact the public safety service that interests you, you find that it does not have an affiliated Explorer post, ask if any other young people have expressed an interest in Explorers. Inquire, too, as to whether any specific officers (or firefighters or EMTs) have shown an interest in Explorers and whether the department as a whole is interested in the program. It is important to do both of these things because you must have potential student members *and* potential adult leaders to start an Explorer post.

If you find a lack of interest on one end, don't give up immediately. Your high school may provide a number of potential members if you orchestrate a publicity campaign carefully explaining the Explorers program and the career you wish to explore as a post. This can be done via your school newspaper, posters, leaflets, announcements, and word of mouth. On the other hand, if you know a few other potential members, you can all prepare a letter or presentation about the Explorers program and your career goals for the public safety department concerned. With a better understanding of what's involved, the department may be more inclined to form a post.

Ultimately, you may find that Explorers is just not an option in your community. The lack of interest may be too serious a problem, or you may find your efforts hampered by those infamous state and local age requirements. But don't let your new contacts in the police, fire, or EMS departments go to waste! Ask them about other programs you might be able to join and other suggestions about what you can do right now. And read on for still more ideas.

TRAINING FOR INTELLIGENCE CAREERS

No, the FBI doesn't have a training program for high school students. But the CIA does. And so do the U.S. Departments of State and Defense. While some of these are aimed at graduating seniors who want to kick-start their postsecondary careers, others are for teenagers who want to work in intelligence *now*. You won't be sent to exotic locales or entrusted with secrets vital to national security, but you will be serving the government—and you might be embarking on a promising career.

The Central Intelligence Agency

The CIA has developed its Undergraduate Scholar Program for minority and disabled high school seniors planning to enter a four- or five-year college program. Those accepted into the program become part of America's foreign intelligence effort by working for the CIA full-time every summer of their undergraduate career. Transportation to and from Washington, DC is provided along with a housing allowance. Participants receive a yearly salary, college tuition up to $15,000 annually, and a full-time position with the agency upon graduation from college.

To qualify, you must be a U.S. citizen, eighteen years of age by April 1 of your senior year, in need of financial assistance for college tuition, and planning to major in computer science, economics, electrical engineering, foreign area studies, or non-Romance foreign languages. Furthermore, you must have a GPA of 2.75 or higher (on a 4.0 scale) and SAT scores of at least 1000 or ACT scores of at least 21. While taking part in the program, you must maintain a GPA of 2.75 or higher in college and meet the same performance standards as CIA employees in comparable positions.

Needless to say, this opportunity in foreign intelligence is highly desirable and therefore very competitive. For you to be considered, the CIA must receive your cover letter, resume, and a copy of your current high school transcript with standardized test scores by November 1 of your senior year. There is no application form. All queries and application packets should be addressed to:

CIA Undergraduate Scholar Program
CIA Employment Center
PO Box 12727
Arlington, VA 22209-8727

The U.S. Department of Defense

The part of the U.S. Department of Defense known as the Defense Intelligence Agency sponsors the Undergraduate Training Assistance Program (UTAP) for dynamic, talented high school seniors with a deep interest in and commitment to national security. Each year, a very few applicants are selected to receive the many benefits of UTAP: tuition (up to $17,000 annually) to a four-year degree program at the college or university of your choice; an annual salary to reflect full-time employment during the summer vacation; and a position at the Defense Intelligence Agency after college graduation. Summer and post-graduation employment may be at any one of the following locations: the Defense Intelligence Analysis Center at Bolling Air Force Base; the Navy Yard in Washington, DC; the Pentagon in Arlington, Virginia; the Defense Intelligence Agency offices in Arlington, Virginia; or the Missile and Space Intelligence Center in Huntsville, Alabama.

To be considered for UTAP, you must have a minimum GPA of 3.0 (on a 4.0 scale), ACT scores of at least 27 or SAT scores of at least 1100, and demonstrated financial need. You and your immediate family must be U.S. citizens. Women, members of minority groups, and those with disabilities are strongly encouraged to apply. You must be planning to major in computer science, geography, earth science, or international relations/political studies in conjunction with a foreign language. These majors represent the areas in which the Defense Intelligence Agency has the greatest need of personnel and they determine where and in what kind of position you will be placed.

If selected for the Undergraduate Training Assistance Program, you must attend university full-time during the school year (maintaining a 3.0 GPA or better on a 4.0 scale) and work full-time for the agency in the summer. You are also obligated to work for the agency for a period one and a half times as long as your period of study (i.e., six years); otherwise, you must reimburse the tuition costs in cash.

This is clearly a demanding and competitive program, but one that offers fantastic opportunities to selected students. Application forms should be available from your guidance counselor, or you can request them from the Defense Intelligence Agency directly. Applicants should submit their materials between October 1 and January 10 of their senior year.

▮Defense Intelligence Agency
Undergraduate Training Assistance Program
Civilian Personnel Division (DAH-2)
Washington, DC 20340-5100

The U.S. Department of State

The U.S. Department of State offers several different opportunities for promising high school students to explore and pursue careers in foreign policy and international relations. Applicants to all of these programs must be U.S. citizens and must pass a background investigation. Competition is tight, so apply as far in advance of your expected start date as possible.

The Summer Clerical Program gives young people office support positions in which they gain work experience and a better understanding of how the State Department works. Participants work during the summer and over the holidays. Applications are due by February 1 in the year in which you wish to begin work.

The Stay-in-School Program is designed for students who require financial assistance to continue their education. In this program, you may work in technical, clerical, or administrative positions part-time during the school year or full-time during the holidays and summer vacation. Contact your guidance counselor or state Employment Service to learn more about the financial criteria.

Finally, the State Department offers a Cooperative Education (Co-op) Program, which integrates and coordinates academic studies with on-the-job experience. Co-op opportunities are available from high school through graduate school; contact your school co-op coordinator (probably your guidance counselor) for more details.

Student Employment Programs
U.S. Department of State
PO Box 9317
Arlington, VA 22219
Tel: 703-875-7490

VICA

VICA stands for the Vocational Industrial Clubs of America, which bills itself as "the national organization for students in trade, industrial, technical, and health occupations education." Yes, VICA is for young people studying these kinds of occupations, among which is law enforcement. The catch is the word "studying," which means that you must be taking a vocational-technical course of study designed to prepare you for your chosen career. VICA is not for high school students who are just thinking about studying law enforcement or who are pursuing that career via a standard college prep curriculum.

If you are pursuing a vocational-technical course in law enforcement and your vo-tech program is affiliated with VICA, you probably already know about the benefits of being involved. But if you've heard about VICA and think it's not worth your time and effort, think again! The Vocational Industrial Clubs of America really is a nationally recognized association with years of experience in preparing young people for the world of work. VICA works with vo-tech programs to improve students' skills, motivation, and understanding of the whole career field they have chosen. Few programs and organizations can give you that kind of help.

One of VICA's most high-profile activities is the annual Skills USA Championships. This competition encourages members to apply themselves to their studies and demonstrate their accomplishments. Beginning at the state level and continuing on to the national level, participants put their skills and knowledge to the test by competing against each other and established time limits.

Law enforcement students are challenged on their ability to explain such crucial concepts as the code of ethics, criminal law, search and seizure regulations, and liabilities. They must also demonstrate their capability to properly approach a suspect vehicle, handcuff criminals, and lift fingerprints, among other things. Those who win at the state level progress to the national competition, and a select few go on to international competition.

Speak with the head of the vo-tech program at your school for more information about VICA. If your school is currently unaffiliated with VICA, you may be able to work with your principal and guidance counselor to establish affiliation, if there is enough interest among other students.

Meeting the People and Learning the Work

This section offers a number of career exploration and preparation opportunities covering most of the public safety field. These activities don't represent career paths as direct as those in the last section, where participants could be associates of a fire department or guarantee themselves a job with the CIA. What's listed in this section are suggestions for getting to know people already working in public safety and experiencing the kinds of duties they perform on a daily basis.

These kinds of activities can be useful to you no matter what your personal situation. If you're confident about your career choice, they'll allow you to learn first-hand about the job you'll be doing as an adult and about the people you'll be working with. If you're still unsure about your career choice, these activities will allow you to make a more informed decision, without requiring the dedication and time commitments of programs like Explorers.

You can be involved in more than one of these activities, and you have some flexibility in deciding when and how often you will participate. At least some of the activities listed here are available in almost every community around the country. And as always, you can use the suggestions here to form ideas and activities of your own, creating opportunities tailored to your interests and your community's needs.

Emergency Medical Services

It can be difficult to get hands-on experience for a career as an Emergency Medical Technician or paramedic because the age and certification requirements in this field tend to be especially strict. However, virtually every community offers high school students the opportunity to work with health care professionals and learn how to care for the sick and injured.

Medical Volunteer Work

Though often associated with preparation for careers in nursing, volunteering at a hospital (or "candystriping," as it is often called) is fantastic preparation for careers in emergency medical services. Almost all hospitals—public and private, general, children's and veterans'—use volunteers to perform routine health care tasks. This not only gives them a chance to explore medical careers, it also gives the nurses and doctors more time to perform complicated and specialized tasks.

Because this kind of volunteer work is so common, it will be easy for you to get started. Simply call the hospital where you would like to work and tell the receptionist who answers that you are interested in volunteering; your call will then be forwarded to a volunteer coordinator or a volunteer association. The person in charge of the volunteer program will tell you the age and other requirements (generally, you must be at least thirteen or fourteen) and will explain the training procedures.

Training procedures vary widely, but a few generalizations can be made. You may train either one-on-one with a nurse or volunteer coordinator, or in a group with other new volunteers. You're likely to train one-on-one if you start during the school year and in a group if your volunteering is part of a summer program. The training may last a couple of hours or a couple of days, depending on the size and scope of the hospital's operations and on the duties you will be expected to carry out.

In general, you can expect to learn how to feed patients, take temperatures, assist patients who have difficulty walking, run errands between wards, and get supplies. If you are to work in a pediatrics ward, you will learn special child care skills. Once you are trained, you and the volunteer coordinator will work out a regular schedule and you can then get to work! Not only will your health care skills be put to the test, but you will also see just how well you cope with people who are unwell and need all your patience and compassion.

In addition to hospitals, you can usually find similar volunteer positions at nursing homes and hospices. You might also want to seek formal instruction in caring for the sick and injured by taking a CPR or First Aid class; details are listed in the section, "Gaining Skills and Strengths."

FIRE FIGHTING

Fire fighting is such a dangerous job that comparatively few communities allow young people to take an active part in it. But like most people working for the public safety, firefighters find their work rewarding and are happy to encourage young people to consider it as a career. Your local fire department, whether volunteer or professional, may have a program that gets teenagers involved with the firefighters. Or, you may be able to arrange a tour of the fire station for yourself or your class. Call your fire department and tell them of your interest.

Teaching Fire Safety to Others
It's likely that when you were a small child, a local firefighter—or even a whole fire engine crew—came to your elementary school to teach you about fire safety. That's where you learned the famous stop-drop-and-roll fire extinguishing technique! Could you now help your fire department put on its fire safety presentations? Could you help them show a filmstrip, distribute pamphlets to the students, assist in their demonstrations of stop-drop-and-roll? This would involve getting permission to miss a couple of your own classes, but it certainly would be a great opportunity to meet the firefighters and share fire safety tips with others. Again, call your local fire department to discuss the possibility.

If the department welcomes your help, you might also want to consider jointly planning fire safety presentations for junior and senior high school students. You know what people in these age groups find interesting and you could suggest creative ways of presenting basic safety guidelines. These ideas—and the concept of a high school student being involved with the presentation—might be new to your fire department, but if you demonstrate your sincere interest in public safety, the firefighters are likely to at least consider them.

Fire Drills and Escape Plans
You might also be able to work with your fire department and your school on the fire drills and fire escape plans set up for you and your classmates. These elements are crucial to everyone's safety, but they are often a bit mysterious. How are fire drills organized? How often are they held? How are fire escape plans made? When are they revised or reviewed? How thoroughly are escape procedures explained to students and teachers? How often are fire alarms and extinguishers checked for problems? And who's in charge of all this? If your principal or a firefighter can take the time to answer all these questions, you'll have received a real education!

But you may be able to do more than ask questions. Once you've found out who's in charge, find out if that person needs an assistant—and volunteer for the job! You'll learn more about fire safety while actually helping to protect others. If your school's administration just isn't ready to take you on as an assistant, remember that it's because their top concern is also public safety. They may be following state safety guidelines, they may want to have just one person bear the responsibility, or they may simply want only adults involved.

LAW ENFORCEMENT

Getting to know your local police department is a vital part of public safety in general and of your career preparations in particular. Various community programs allow you to develop friendly relationships with police officers and act as their eyes and ears when they can't be around in person. Your purpose in such programs is to prevent crimes from occurring and to solve them once they do. You therefore share the same goals as police officers and, in a limited way, also share their work.

Bicycle Registration and Safety

This isn't a glamorous crime-fighting activity, but it *is* a great way to assist your local police department and contribute to public safety. In many, if not most, communities, the police register the bicycles of young children so that they can be identified in case of theft or accident. Police are also often responsible for presentations and brochures that teach kids about bicycle safety, particularly riding bicycles alongside automobile traffic. If your local law enforcement agency does this kind of work, why not volunteer to help? On a bicycle registration day, you might help with record-keeping, directing children to the right areas, distributing literature, or assisting the officers on duty. If officers are planning presentations at local malls or schools, you might assist there, too. Simply contact your police department.

Neighborhood Watch and Community Policing

These are two programs that will not only keep you in touch with your local police department, they'll also make the area where you live a safer place. Neighborhood Watch is a well-established program in which community residents are trained to recognize and report suspicious activities *before* actual crimes are committed. Of course, they also report crimes that are in progress or completed, but the ideal is to alert police before violence and damage is done and while the suspects are still on the scene.

The success of the program hinges on the cooperation between local law enforcement and the community. The volunteer neighborhood coordinator is assisted by a number of volunteer block captains and all of the block watchers who agree to look out for the safety of their neighbors. Block captains host Neighborhood Watch meetings, often monthly, which bring together their block watchers and liaisons from the police department. The law enforcement officers provide all Neighborhood Watch participants with literature and other information on identifying suspicious activities and making their homes and valuables more secure.

If your community has a Neighborhood Watch program, it's well worth getting involved. Try to join the program with your entire household, so that you are all trained and ready to act for the public safety. If there is no Neighborhood Watch in your community, contact the police department to see about starting one; it doesn't take very much money or time to run the program, and there are many model programs around the country that can give you ideas and tips on getting started. Check with the cities around you.

Community policing doesn't give you the chance to meet with local police officers on a regular basis or do quite so much crime fighting. It is a relatively new concept that has police officers permanently patrolling the same small area, often on foot. The goal is to acquaint the officer and neighborhood residents with each other, developing a sense of trust and friendship, and again alerting police to suspicious activities before they evolve into crimes. If community policing has been introduced in your area, get to know the patrol officer and do your part to keep him or her informed about what's going on in the neighborhood. This is an opportunity to develop a special friendship with a law enforcement officer.

Police Athletic Leagues (PALs)

If you're really interested in meeting police officers, find out if your community has a Police Athletic League. Instead of sitting around the house with your friends, you can all be outside playing football or basketball with your town's own law enforcement officers! PALs keep young people busy and encourage them to take police officers as their role models. This means that you'll have the opportunity to find out what it's *really* like to work in law enforcement from the people who know.

If you take your sports almost as seriously as you take public safety, you'll feel right at home with the Police Athletic Leagues. They sponsor competitions at the regional and state level, so you can really work on your game—whatever it is. The National Association of PALs even sponsors national tournaments in basketball, baseball, and ice hockey. Girls are welcome in PALs and there's even a national girls' softball tournament.

Scholastic Crime Stoppers

You've probably heard of Crime Stoppers International, which focuses on unsolved crimes and asks ordinary citizens to anonymously phone in tips and leads, with reward money available if a conviction is secured. Scholastic Crime Stoppers is a student branch of that organization, focusing primarily on high schools. Members of Scholastic Crime Stoppers work with school administrators to set up and run a similar anonymous-tip-and-reward program within their high schools. They send a clear message: teenagers will not tolerate crime.

Of course, that's just the kind of message *you* want to send—so consider getting involved with your school's Scholastic Crime Stoppers program or starting one of your own. Students run the program's board of directors at their school, reviewing information about crimes already committed, raising and allotting reward money, and publicizing the program among their peers. The names of victims, witnesses, and suspects are not known to boards of directors, only to school administrators. From hotlines to video reenactments, Scholastic Crime Stoppers groups use every method their creativity can devise to accomplish their goals. You can get involved, take on a leadership or supporting role, and make your school a safer place.

If your school doesn't already have a Scholastic Crime Stoppers group, contact the man who runs the program for Crime Stoppers International for information about starting one.

■ Scholastic Crime Stoppers
c/o Larry Wieda
4441 Prairie Trail Drive
Loveland, CO 80537
Tel: 303-441-3327
Fax: 303-441-4327

GAINING SKILLS AND STRENGTHS

If you are still having trouble finding ways to prepare for a career in public safety or if you feel the other preparations you're making just aren't enough, there are still more activities you should consider—and they're available almost everywhere. Best of all, the skills and strengths taught and improved by the listings below will be useful to you no matter what career you finally decide upon. So, even if you feel that something like Explorers is too much of a commitment to public safety careers, you can plunge into *these* activities fearlessly!

TAKING CLASSES

You may not be very enthusiastic about taking even more classes than your high school requires, but they can put you at a real advantage in the years to come. Actually, many of the courses suggested here are probably offered by your school, so you can gain credit for them and not take on an extra burden. Or you may have the chance to take these classes at a local college, public library, or community center—all of which can be great new opportunities for you.

Academics and Athletics

Computers have long been used by state and federal public safety agencies, but today, even some of the smallest municipal police departments and fire stations are using them in their work. Since you can expect to use computers in at least some aspects of your future career (chiefly record-keeping and correspondence), why not learn to use them now? Basic typing and word processing skills, simple Internet navigation, and the use of databases to store information are important skills in this and almost every field. Your school probably offers some computer classes, but if not, a local library, college, or community center is likely to. And if you get beyond the basics, you'll be at a real advantage when applying to colleges or employers.

For most public safety careers, the knowledge of a foreign language is a real asset—and depending on exactly what kind of job you want, it may be a requirement. After all, won't a basic command of Spanish make you a more effective border patrol guard? And is the State Department likely to send you on an exciting overseas assignment if you can't converse with the natives or read the newspapers? Fortunately, your school almost certainly offers foreign language classes you can take now. If you're particularly interested in a language not offered in school, your public library or local community college should be able to give you some leads, even if they don't offer classes themselves.

Common sense—and the career articles earlier in the book—make it clear that most people working in the public safety field must have achieved a considerable degree of physical fitness. No, you don't have to be a star athlete, but you must be agile and quick enough to carry out your duties and not needlessly endanger your own safety. You can get a jump on the exercise and fitness requirements that you're certain to encounter later by becoming more active now. It can be as simple as walking regularly in a nearby park, swimming twice a week at the YMCA, or joining an intramural sport at school. Consult a professional organization or Web site connected to the career that interests you to get some specifics on the fitness requirements.

Please note that people with physical disabilities are not barred from pursuing public safety careers. If you are concerned about certain duties performed in a specific job like EMT or Secret Service agent, discuss the situation with a related professional organization or your own guidance counselor.

First Aid and Beyond

Regardless of which public safety career interests you, you should seriously consider taking a class in First Aid or CPR—or both. Your local Red Cross, YMCA, or hospital most likely offers this kind of training for a reasonable fee. CPR and First Aid skills are of vital importance to every law enforcement officer, firefighter, and of course, emergency medical technician, and you can get a head start. But before you actually begin your career—and even if you eventually decide not to go into public safety at all—CPR and First Aid courses will allow you to react promptly and effectively to medical emergencies around you. How should you react if a teacher faints in class? What should you do if a classmate cuts herself badly in industrial arts? If you've taken the proper courses, you'll know.

Besides First Aid and CPR, the Red Cross offers a number of courses and programs that are worth exploring. After all, what single organization does more for public safety than they do? They can provide you with the training needed to educate your peers and your community about HIV/AIDS, staying healthy, swimming and water safety, and how to respond to disasters. Each local Red Cross office has different programs available, so call the one nearest you to see what it offers for teenagers. You might also want to check out the Red Cross's extensive Web site—which will help you locate the office in your area—at http://www.redcross.org.

BUILDING CHARACTER

If there's one thing that sounds less appealing than taking extra classes, it's probably building character! That's because building character has a bad rap, thanks to those adults who automatically associate it with all the chores and responsibilities young people don't like. But character building is no bad thing; you've probably found for yourself that facing up to new and challenging situations generally does make you a stronger and more capable person. And the bottom line is that no one is more in demand in the field of public safety than the strong and capable person.

As important as skills and work experience are, your character is paramount in establishing how effective you will be as a public safety worker, and it is likely to considerably influence what kind of employer will hire you. Public safety organizations can teach you how to hold a fire hose or analyze finger-prints, for example, but only you can determine the quality of your character. Intelligence agencies in particular demand evidence of their employees' good character—and that goes well beyond not having a criminal record. So what kind of evidence can you offer? The activities you pursue in your free time speak volumes about your character.

Since every public safety career is one of service to the community, the best way to spend at least some of your free time is in service to others. But this doesn't have to mean drudgery or work that is unfulfilling to you. On the contrary, there are so many service options that you are certain to find one you'll enjoy almost as much as the people you're helping!

Serving the Community

Probably one of the first community service options that comes to mind is working with the less fortunate: the poor, the sick, the neglected. Your city's Department of Health and Human Services, your school system, and your church or temple are all likely to run programs to help these people—and they're all likely to welcome your involvement. It may take only a few hours a week or one Saturday a month to collect clothes for needy children, take food to the house-bound elderly, or mow the lawn for a person who has difficulty walking. And if you can't find a service program that appeals to you or if you see a need for a program that doesn't yet exist, work with one of the institutions listed above and start your own. That shows initiative *and* character!

Other ways to build character through public service include working to improve the environment and supporting charitable organizations. You don't have to take on environmental issues of global proportions like the green-house effect or rainforest destruction—although you're certainly welcome to do so! But in your own community, whether it's large or small, there are recy-cling issues, pollution problems, and threatened habitats that need your help. You may choose to work with an established environmental group or on your own as a concerned citizen. Either way, you are performing a valuable service for all your neighbors—and all those of the future.

Charitable organizations are, of course, often an intrinsic part of help-ing the less fortunate and working for environmental protection. However, you can be of service to any number of charities concerned with other community issues: education, religious and political causes, the fine arts, science, history, sports, and many more. Your involvement doesn't have to involve financial contributions at all: the donation of your time is most valuable to the charities and to your career goals.

All of these things demonstrate your interest in and commitment to people and values besides yourself. And, sure enough, the new situations and challenges you'll encounter in these activities really will build up your character! Your involvement shows your good character and your commitment to public service to colleges and employers more clearly than any application form or essay ever could.

FINALLY . . .

Regardless of which public safety activities you're able to become involved with right now, make sure you're doing _something_. Your interest in this career field is important because the tasks done by public safety workers are so vital and good workers are so essential. That's obviously true of policing and fire fighting, but it is equally true of lower-profile jobs in corrections and intelligence. Should your career explorations prove that public safety isn't the right field for you, you will nevertheless have gained new friends, new skills, and a new appreciation of the men and women who keep us safe and secure.

BY THE WAY

Throughout this section, we offer suggestions on who to contact to get involved with the public safety programs on offer. Usually, the contact is the EMS, fire, or police department in your own neighborhood; occasionally, we give you the name and address of a national organization. But when you're ready to contact someone, what should you actually _do_?

If you want to speak with one of the public safety services in your community, do _not_ call 911! That number is exclusively for emergencies. Instead, look in the telephone book: either the inside front cover or the blue "Government" pages will give you the regular business phone numbers you need. If you know for certain that they have a program you want to join (perhaps Explorers or the Police Athletic League), simply ask to speak to the person in charge of that program. If you're not after a specific program or not sure what they offer, just explain who you are and why you are calling. It's a good idea to write this out before getting on the telephone. That makes things clear in your own mind and ensures that you don't confuse or waste the time of the person who answers your call.

Once you figure out exactly who you need to speak with, you may well find that he or she is out on the job. Leave your name, telephone number, and a brief message about the reason for your call, asking the person to call you back. If your call is not returned in a few days, try again! Be persistent until you make personal contact; after all, it's your future we're talking about. When you finally do make contact, be very clear and direct about what you're interested in. Again, it can really help to write up a few sentences beforehand, and you may also want to note any pressing questions you want answered.

If you're contacting a national organization, it's again important to be very specific about what you want from them: more information, the address of a local branch, an application packet, etc. Your request may be complex enough to warrant a carefully written letter instead of a phone call; use your own judgment, and remember that writing things out really helps to clarify them.

Finally, no matter who you are calling or writing, always do it yourself. Don't let Mom or Dad do it for you. If you want to prepare for your adult life, if you want to take charge of your future, start now. If *you* want to get involved, *you* have to get in touch.

Surf the Web

FIRST

You *must* use the Internet to do research, to find out, to explore. The Internet is the closest you'll get to what's happening right now all around the world. This chapter gets you started with an annotated list of Web sites related to public safety. Try a few. Follow the links. Maybe even venture as far as asking questions in a chat room. The more you read about and interact with public safety personnel, the better prepared you'll be when you're old enough to participate as a professional.

One caveat: you probably already know that URLs change all the time. If a Web address listed below is out of date, try searching on the site's name or other key words. Chances are, if it's still out there, you'll find it. If it's not, maybe you'll find something better!

BELLINGHAM HIGH SCHOOL ONLINE

http://wwwbhs1.bham.wednet.edu/he_links.htm

This site comes to you from Bellingham, Washington, where high school students have amassed some excellent career information and put it on-line. Careers are broken into categories, which are then further broken down into skilled, technical, and professional categories—with recommended high school courses for each. Under the heading of Human Services and Education, one of the careers you can read about is police officer. There's a well-written report by a student who is working as a junior police officer, along with other factual information. Other relevant careers profiled here included corrections officer and FBI agent. You can do a little backtracking to the Career Pathways museum if you want to evaluate your personality to see if it matches up with careers profiles. There's also an Online Career Center, with links to the

131

Occupational Outlook Handbook and several resources for finding scholarships and other financial aid.

BUREAU OF ALCOHOL, TOBACCO, AND FIREARMS
http://www.atf.treas.gov/

The Bureau of Alcohol, Tobacco, and Firearms (ATF) has put together an extremely informative site. Naturally, each one of the bureau's concerns has its own section. The Frequently Asked Questions (FAQ) pages in these sections will tell you all you'll ever want to know about the ATF. For information that could affect your high school career, click on Outreach, a gold mine of information about the Gang Resistance Education and Training (GREAT) Program. Thousands of law enforcement officers, including many in the ATF, have been trained to present this gang prevention curriculum in classrooms. There's also a description here of how the Department of Justice (ATF's boss) helped establish the Academy of Law, Justice, and Security in 1991, a school-within-a school at Anacostia High School in Washington, DC. This is one of about one hundred and fifty career academies that try to prevent students from joining gangs by offering some of the same things youth seek from gangs: a sense of belonging, peer support, a perceived future, and a way to make a living.

THE CENTER FOR FORENSICS STUDIES
http://www.phys.ttu.edu/~menzel/

This site will plunge you headfirst into criminalistics (also known as crime analysis or criminology). Located at Texas Tech University, the center strives to put cutting-edge technology to use in crime analysis. You'll read about methods like photoluminescence detection of latent fingerprints and even see some photos. The site also describes workshops that are conducted for law enforcement personnel in order to get them up to speed on the newest research. Another piece of the center's work is conducting case examinations for smaller law enforcement agencies that can't afford the pricey equipment that's needed. The center soon hopes to offer a forensic science and technology degree program. Currently, both undergraduate and graduate students work on criminalistics research projects at the center while earning their degrees in another field, usually sciences or engineering. You can read the resumes of the staff and students at the center and learn a ton about laser fingerprinting. If you're really, really interested in fingerprints, explore some of the expanded literature and scientific diagrams. The center has also compiled some excellent links to other forensics-related sites, such as the American Society of Crime Laboratory Directors.

THE CENTRAL INTELLIGENCE AGENCY (CIA)

http://www.odci.gov/cia/

The CIA's site just isn't as user-friendly as the FBI's. There's a virtual tour of the agency's headquarters, but you have to fish through a section called "About the CIA" to find it. And once you're on the tour, you only get to see photos of the lobby, several statues, a courtyard, and a monument—in other words, you're still kept at arm's length from the interior of the CIA. One exception to this otherwise guarded site is the employment section, which describes some juicy internships, co-op opportunities, and scholarships for college undergraduates. In this section, you'll also find a Job Kit and Resume Guide to help you prepare an electronic resume for consideration by the CIA. And you can browse through the amazing variety of positions within the CIA, such as language instructor, economist, leather and fabric crafts specialist, and theater effects specialist.The rest of the site is broken into CIA Publications/Handbooks and Public Affairs (press releases and speeches). In Publications, you'll find some useful reference tools such as the World Factbook, the Factbook on Intelligence, and a suggested reading list of intelligence literature.

COLD CASE: TRUE CRIME INVESTIGATIONS

http://www.coldcase.com/

In case you didn't catch this program on CBS Television, here's the Web site where you can assist in solving actual murder cases. The format follows that of a homicide detective's "murder book" that is prepared during the course of an investigation and maintained during the trial. It's divided into a case overview, incident reports, crime scene, witness statements, autopsy reports, and forensics. Some of the cases offer rewards that could put you through four years of college. You can click on any of the file folders to begin your investigation. If you don't want to tie up your modem line, simply download an entire case folder. Should you have a question or maybe even a lead in the case, you can click on an email link to the lead investigator for the case. This site is extremely well organized, interesting to navigate through, and only occasionally ventures into the sensationalistic.

THE COMMUNITY POLICING CONSORTIUM

http://www.communitypolicing.org/

This site is sponsored by a partnership of five leading police groups that are committed to the development of community policing: the International Association of Chiefs of Police (IACP), the National Organization of Black Law Enforcement Executives (NOBLE), the National Sheriffs' Association (NSA), the Police Executive Research Forum (PERF), and the Police Foundation. Naturally, you'll be able to read extensively about the progressive philosophy of community policing here. In short, it revolves around encouraging police officers to become partners with their communities and allowing them to spend more time on the street, instead of behind a desk. If you decide to explore the topic or perhaps write a paper on it, the "Publications" section offers some very readable and engaging texts and speeches. It's also interesting to read the "Bulletin Board," where police officers have expressed their ideas and experiences about community policing. This is a revealing peek into the glory and the frustration of police work. This is a fully developed site, with training information and lots of links to other sites on community policing.

CoolWorks

http://www.coolworks.com/showme

You've probably had a time of it trying to find a summer job that's fun *and* relevant to your future career of law enforcement. CoolWorks quickly links you up to a mass of information about seasonal security jobs at dozens of national and state parks, preserves, monuments, and wilderness areas. There are also listings of jobs and volunteer opportunities at ski areas, private resorts, cruise ships, and summer camps. Most of the national and state jobs require that applicants be eighteen years or older. Most national and state parks listed here have seasonal positions available in similar departments. Specific job descriptions can also be accessed by clicking on a location that interests you on the USA Job Map. The map links to comprehensive descriptions of the park's attractions, facilities, and jobs currently available. You can also check out where recruiters for some of the larger parks and resorts will be traveling. If planning ahead isn't your forte, look to the "Help Wanted Now" listings for immediate job openings. While only a handful of jobs allow you to apply directly on-line, many have downloadable application forms.

THE CORRECTIONS CONNECTION

http://www.corrections.com/

Voted Microsoft's Outstanding Justice Web Site, the Corrections Connection is the largest on-line resource for corrections. You'll find everything from corrections associations and industry publications to chatrooms and research libraries to legislative updates. There's a very useful Student Center where you can submit questions about any topic related to corrections or about finding an internship, and someone working in the field will answer it. Many of the questions posted are from college students writing research papers or seeking summer jobs. There's also a listing of the email addresses of professionals who are willing to be contacted by students. In another section called the Career Center, there's a special place for recent college graduates who are looking for work in corrections to post their resumes. This site might open your eyes to the variety of people working in prisons. For instance, there's actually a whole section devoted to food services and another to correctional technology.

FEDERAL BUREAU OF INVESTIGATION
http://www.fbi.gov/

Even though this site's welcome message says upfront that the information is unclassified and for educational purposes, what you do find here is surprisingly weighty. Those considering a career as a special agent will learn plenty by combing these pages. An incredibly useful section called "99 Frequently Asked Questions" provides background information about the FBI's mission and structure, plus specific employment-related information on jobs and necessary qualifications. Other questions pertain to specific areas of investigation within the FBI, such as counterterrorism, organized crime, and foreign counterintelligence. You'll also want to look at the list of the FBI's 56 field offices (where most of the hiring occurs) and click on individual home pages to find out more about the location closest to you. Another section is devoted to the FBI Academy, with information on new agent training. Read it to decide if you're up to the rigors of the fifteen-week training, which includes academics, firearms, physical training/defensive tactics, and practical exercises. Crime buffs will enjoy delving into the FBI Case Files, which contain unclassified collections of letters, newspaper stories, and investigative data on high-profile figures like Elvis Presley and Amelia Earhart. Overall, this is a straightforward, easy-to-browse site. If it stimulates your interest in the FBI and you decide to visit its headquarters in the flesh, you can even arrange for a guided tour here.

FEDERAL LAW ENFORCEMENT CAREER RESOURCES
http://www.concentric.net/~extraord/law.htm

The home page speaks for itself: "If you are interested in a law enforcement career or simply want to find out more about the different federal law enforce-

WHAT CAN I DO RIGHT NOW?

ment agencies, then this page is for you." In a section focusing on the major federal law enforcement agencies—such as the U.S. Secret Service, the FBI, and the Immigration and Naturalization Service—there are short-but-sweet descriptions of the nature of the work at each agency. An employment opportunities section provides two links: one to all of the federal job openings and another to jobs at the state, county, and municipal level. A books database will find information on just about any book related to law enforcement. You can search by title, author, keyword, or subject. And to try out your crime analysis skills, the Solve-a-Crime section links you to about a dozen sites where you can help law enforcement officials solve actual crimes. The webmaster has taken the time to not only create links to many other sites, but describe them in rich detail. You'll enjoy the lighthearted tone of this site, complemented by solid, valuable information. Whether it's hard-core career information you need or just some fun, you'll find it here.

FIREFIGHTING.COM
http://www.firefighting.com/

This is a huge site for firefighters and emergency medical workers, with an uncountable number of somewhat confusing sections and subsections. Feel free to explore the whole site or just take a look at a few of the highlights, like "Hook," a massive photo archive of historic firehouses, horse-drawn equipment, and more. You'll want to read the site's Guestbook, a compilation of firefighters' revelations and stories. Many of these entries describe personal crises in their own families and ask for moral support. You'll come away with a strong impression of a thriving on-line community of emergency rescue personnel. Elsewhere, a section called "10/75" will take you to an entirely separate—and equally labyrinthian—site that has a job search database, relevant news headlines, and live chat rooms. FireFighting.Com's poor organization is a strike against it, but it's got far more information than most other emergency medical services sites—including fresh touches like poems penned by firefighters.

FORENSIC SCIENCES STUDENT ORGANIZATION
http://gwis.circ.gwu.edu/~forensic/

George Washington University's forensic science department is in the spotlight here. This department was created at the request of former FBI Director J. Edgar Hoover, and originally, all the classes were conducted at FBI headquarters. Since then, the department has moved on campus, but it still works closely with the FBI to educate and train agents. If you're thinking of becoming a crime analyst, you may decide to study forensics in college. The site says that students in GWU's program graduate with degrees as varied as forensic chemistry, toxicology, biology, criminal justice, and security management. Because of the department's close ties to several local and federal agencies, good internships are available to many of its students. Unfortunately, much of the information here is directed at students shopping for graduate programs. But you should be able to glean a few ideas and if nothing else, there are excellent links to other forensics sites, including some unusually specialized ones like forensic photography and forensic entomology.

K9 HOMEPAGE
http://www.best.com/~policek9/k9home.htm

If law enforcement and dogs are your two great loves, then this site is your nirvana. It's sponsored by the K9 Academy for Law Enforcement, and it has extensive information on the training and use of police dogs. Some of the information is probably more in-depth than is necessary, like the demonstration of software used in training a police dog (bet you didn't know such a thing existed). But you might enjoy reading about the International Police K9 Conference, which brings the world's best instructors together to train dogs in safer police work. From the home page, you can link to other K9 associations and see if there's a K9 unit at a station near you. If you're really interested in the subject, you'll want to read the on-line training manuals that throw around phrases like "clean bitework" and "canine pheromones."

THE 911 FIRE POLICE MEDICAL WEB SITE
http://www.hotcity.com/911/

Although you can navigate through this site pretty quickly and easily, you should plan on spending a lot of time here: there is just too much information and too many good links to see on a quick visit. As its name advertises, the 911 Fire Police Medical Web site covers work in fire fighting, law enforcement, and emergency medical services. It also features coverage of severe weather events and other disasters as they occur—very sensible, considering that they require the response of all the emergency services and several other public safety organizations besides. The 911 Fire Police Medical Web site offers sone articles and features of its own, but its outstanding characteristic is its links to other sites. At the time of the writing of this book, it had easy-to-follow links to over seven hundred fire departments in the U.S.A. and Canada and more than 2000 links to general emergency services ranging from 77 sheriff's departments to 127

EMS 911 dispatchers. There are also links to fire fighting brigades around the world and to various on-line public safety newsletters. It's hard to imagine any emergency services information you couldn't find via this Web site.

THE POLICE OFFICER'S INTERNET DIRECTORY
http://www.officer.com/

You won't find a more valuable, inclusive home page for law enforcement information. This well-organized site is broken into fourteen jam-packed sub-directories, such as associations and organizations, employment, wanted files and crime stoppers, training opportunities, and criminal justice resources. It's hard to believe, but a lone police officer maintains this site. One subdirectory that might be of particular use to you is the directory of law officers' home pages, where an astonishing number of officers have posted information about themselves, their jobs, and their departments. Many of these people are willing to be contacted about career opportunities. You can easily search this section since the names are organized alphabetically by state. This would be a great place to find a local police officer who's willing to tell you more about the field. Another unique feature is the topical index at the bottom of the home page. Here, you could learn about more obscure topics like "citizen academies" and "patch collecting."

THE PRINCETON REVIEW
http://www.review.com/

This site is everything you want in a high school guidance counselor—it's friendly, well-informed, and available to you night and day. Originally a standardized test preparation company, the Princeton Review is now on-line, offering frank advice on colleges, careers, and of course, SATs. You'll find good tips here on how to present your extracurricular activities on college application forms. There's a handy link to *Time*'s interactive guide, "The Best College for You," which discusses costs, admissions, and alternatives to four years of college. If you're looking for contact with other students who are also weighing their options, link to one of the discussion groups on college admissions and careers. Two of the Princeton Review's coolest tools are the Find-O-Rama, which creates a list of schools based on the criteria you type in, and the Counselor-O-Matic, which reviews your grades, test scores, and extracurricular record to calculate your chances of admission at many colleges.

TRIPOD: INTERNSHIPS

http://www.tripod.com/work/internships/

Tripod is a magazine-style Web site that focuses on four broad topics: work, money, living, and health. You'll want to beeline toward the work section, where you can search the latest edition of the National Directory of Internships, which was created by the National Society of Experiential Education. You conduct your search by simply picking a career category from a long list, then selecting a geographic region. For instance, a search for internships related to criminal justice anywhere in the United States netted internships with the Boulder County Justice System Volunteer Program, the National Crime Prevention Council, and the Vera Institute of Justice, among others. Or you can just search by keywords. For example, type in "police" and "security" and up comes a list of potential internships for you. You'll have to spend about two minutes signing up as an official member, then another five minutes waiting for an email that reveals your secret member password. But what's seven minutes when you're looking for a great job?

USDA FOREST SERVICE

http://www.fs.fed.us/

Did you realize that the Forest Service employs more than seven hundred people to police federal lands and conduct criminal investigations? Scratch beneath the surface of this mostly text-based government site, and you'll find a useful resource about working as a law enforcement officer for the Forest Service. One area in particular, Human Resources, is stuffed with relevant information on job possibilities. Here you'll find links to several job search engines, including the vast FedWorld database. There's also an overview to the kinds of Forest Service jobs there are and how to get one. A section on volunteer opportunities unfortunately listed only one option at the time. You can also access a guide to grants, fellowships, and scholarships that provides detailed descriptions of funding available to university students or professionals. If you're applying for a college scholarship, visit this site for eligibility requirements, deadlines, and contacts.

US NEWS: HOT TRACKS

http://www.usnews.com/usnews/issue/28cor4.htm

This issue's cover story was "The Best Jobs for the Future." In the arena of law enforcement, the career path of a crime analyst was selected as being on the fast track. The International Association of Crime Analysts states here that the demand for these professionals has risen tenfold in the last fifteen years. The on-line article goes on to describe some of the ways that crime analysts use technology—such as computer-mapping software—to analyze the crime data that often leads police to suspects. While there isn't a lot of information at this site, it does cover what you want to know—how much money is to be made, for example. You can see what entry-, mid-, and top-level crime analysts are paid. For comparison, the site also lists the salaries of related jobs, such as police officer, FBI special agent, intelligence analyst, and crime lab director.

THE UNOFFICIAL BORDER PATROL WEB SITE

http://members.aol.com/usbp1/index.htm

This site offers a comprehensive overview of the U.S. Border Patrol's mission, organization, and history. If working for the Border Patrol is your goal, you'll appreciate the step-by-step outline of the hiring process and the description of new agent training. The Border Patrol is, of course, the enforcement arm of the Immigration and Naturalization Service, and its mission is to detect and prevent smuggling and illegal entry of aliens into the United States. This Web site doesn't glamorize the job. It's described as "hours, days, and often months of dull, routine patrol that is occasionally marked with intense action, suspense, and danger." Another section of the site provides an interesting historical perspective and photos of Border Patrol agents—who were first called "mounted inspectors." There is also a section about the issues that affect the northern and southern border patrols, featuring a series of Associated Press articles. In "Current Events," look for frequent updates on hiring, ongoing operations, and other newsworthy events. This site is engaging, well designed, and clearly intended for someone like you who is exploring the career. It'll even teach you some new terminology like "signcutting," a way that Border Patrol pilots spot and follow footprints from the air in order to direct the movement of the ground agents.

VOCAL POINT

http://bvsd.k12.co.us/cent/Newspaper/Newspaper.html

Vocal Point is an electronic student newspaper written, designed, and maintained by students in Boulder, Colorado. The site has received the Cornerstone Foundation Award for "Excellence in Youth Services" and was given a "Thumbs Up" by the Teenager's Circle. What makes this on-line publication stand out is its thoughtful and substantive content. Each issue delves into a single, broad topic such as poverty, violence, or censorship. As an example, the issue focusing on violence included student-written articles about how violence in movies impacts street crime, a look at the frightening rise of white supremacy groups, and an essay that posed the question, "Are There Gangs in My School?" In recent issues, *Vocal Point* has included articles by students from schools in other states, and its editors say they hope to expand to include contributions from overseas as well. You can contact the student editors and designers or the teachers involved via handy email links.

Read a Book

When it comes to finding out about public safety, don't overlook a book. (You're reading one now, after all.) What follows is a short, annotated list of books and periodicals related to public safety. The books range from fiction to personal accounts of what it's like to be a fire fighter or intelligence officer, to professional volumes on specific topics, such as gangs and studying for exams. Don't be afraid to check out the professional journals, either. The technical stuff may be way above your head right now, but if you take the time to become familiar with one or two, you're bound to pick up some of what is important to public safety personnel, not to mention begin to feel like a part of their world, which is what you're interested in, right?

We've tried to include recent materials as well as old favorites. Always check for the most recent editions, and, if you find an author you like, ask your librarian to help you find more. Keep reading good books!

BOOKS

Adams, Sam. *War of Numbers: An Intelligence Memoir.* South Royalton: Steerforth Press, 1994. A fascinating account about a CIA controversy in Vietnam that takes stock of how intelligence may be collected, collated, interpreted, and sometimes ignored.

Andrew, Christopher. *For the President's Eyes Only: Secret Intelligence and American Presidency from Washington to Bush.* New York: Harper Perennial Library, 1996. An insightful book by a leading authority on intelligence history, explaining how the presidency was influenced by the workings of U.S. intelligence.

Bales, Don L. *Correctional Officer Resource Guide.* Lanham: American Correctional Association, 1997. An ideal guide for the aspiring correctional officer, filled with information about where the jobs are and how to get them.

Barkan, Steven E. *Criminology: A Sociological Understanding.* Paramus: Prentice Hall, 1996. An up-to-date textbook that treats social structure and social inequalities as central themes in the study of crime. An essential introduction to crime analysis.

Brown, Larry. *On Fire.* Chapel Hill: Algonquin Books, 1994. A complex and moving memoir, recounting 17 years as a fireman in Oxford, Mississippi.

Butterworth-Heinemann. *Protection Officer Training Manual.* 6th ed. Newton: Butterworth-Heinemann, 1997. A useful and thorough guide to private security service careers and preventive police work.

Camenson, Blythe. *Firefighting.* VGM Career Portraits. Lincolnwood: NTC Publishing Group, 1995. Presents information on the various duties of firefighters, including emergency medical services, fire investigation and prevention, training, and administration.

Delattre, Edwin J. *Character and Cops: Ethics in Policing.* 2nd ed. Kansas City: Aei Press, 1994. An interesting overview of ethical issues in law enforcement and police training in the U.S.

Delsohn, Steve, ed. *The Fire Inside: Firefighters Talk About Their Lives.* New York: HarperCollins, 1996. A wide-ranging collection of stories, interviews, and other information that offers an emotional portrait of these uniquely dedicated public servants.

Dershowitz, Alan M. *The Abuse Excuse: And Other Cop-Outs, Sob Stories, and Evasions of Responsibility.* Boston: Little, Brown Co., 1994. The famous attorney reviews a wide range of cases—including O.J., William Kennedy Smith, and Tonya Harding—discussing issues of criminality, accountability, and justice.

Dunn, William C. *Boot: An LAPD Officer's Rookie Year.* New York: William Morrow & Co., 1996. First-hand reports from the front line of the war on crime in Los Angeles. Shows how a department that has been portrayed as sexist, racist, inept, mismanaged, and unduly brutal is actually composed of dedicated, disciplined professionals who risk their lives with honor.

Ertel, Mike, and Gregory C. Berk. *Firefighting: Basic Skills and Techniques.* South Holland: Goodheart-Willcox Co., 1997. A useful survey of the field, providing the basic guidelines of fire extinction and safety.

Ferrell, Jeff, and Clinton Sanders, eds. *Cultural Criminology*. Boston: Northeastern University Press, 1995. A worthwhile text in the study of crime that collects important essays on how crime relates to various cultural forms—particularly the media.

Fisher, David. *Hard Evidence: How Detectives Inside the FBI's Sci-Crime Lab Have Helped Solve America's Toughest Cases*. New York: Dell Books, 1996. A bestselling author takes readers into the greatest sci-crime lab in the world to show how the FBI adapted space-age science and technology to solve such cases as the bombing of the World Trade Center.

Hammer, Hy, and Edward Scheinkman. *State Trooper: Highway Patrol Officer, State Traffic Officer*. 12th ed. New York: Arco Publishers, 1997. The best preparation available for the tests required in all 50 states. Features four full-length exams and a detailed answer key.

Hammett, Dashiell. *The Big Knockover: Selected Stories and Short Novels*. Edited by Lillian Hellman. New York: Vintage Books, 1994. Sharp, detailed, and gripping stories—by a master storyteller—about revolutionaries, cowboys, and gangsters.

Icove, David J., and Karl A. Seger. *Computer Crime: A Crimefighter's Handbook*. Sebastopol: O'Reilly & Associates, 1995. A fascinating collection of facts about terrorist attacks on computer centers, electronic fraud on funds transfer networks, viruses and worms in our software, network espionage, and the like.

Ivey, Pat. *EMT: Beyond the Lights and Sirens*. New York : Ivy Books, 1991. Real, gritty, and compassionate tales from the life of a volunteer on a rural ambulance squad.

Ivey, Pat. *EMT: Rescue*. New York: Ivy Books, 1993. An excellent sequel to Ivey's first book, offering more true minute-by-minute accounts of mobile rescue.

Jeffreys, Diarmuid. *The Bureau: Inside the Modern FBI*. Boston: Houghton Mifflin Co., 1995. Takes us on a whirlwind tour of the modern FBI. Full of fascinating anecdotes and fresh information; finely detailed, level-headed, and well-written.

Johnson, Loch K. *Secret Agencies: U.S. Intelligence in a Hostile World*. New Haven: Yale University Press, 1996. A former assistant to Defense Secretary Lee Aspin and now a university professor defends intelligence networks from charges of ineptitude and corruption.

Knott, Stephen F. *Secret and Sanctioned: Covert Operations and the American Presidency*. New York: Oxford University Press, 1996. An eye-opening account that reveals that covert intelligence operations in the U.S. date much farther back than most people realize—back to the Founding Fathers.

Landre, Rick, Mike Miller, and Dee Porter. *Gangs: A Handbook for Community Awareness.* New York: Facts on File, 1997. A detailed guide for community that addresses concerns about gang violence, juvenile delinquency, and local crime generally speaking.

Lee, Mary Price, and Richard S. Lee. *Careers in Firefighting.* New York: Rosen Publishing Group, 1993. Explores every detail in the life of a firefighter, discussing such aspects as training, equipment, and related jobs in the field.

Lindsay, Paul. *Code Name: Gentkill: A Novel of the FBI.* New York: Fawcett Gold Medal, 1996. A gripping novel about a serial murderer who is systematically gunning down FBI agents, and the agent who must stop him.

Livingston, Jay. *Crime and Criminology.* 2nd ed. Paramus: Prentice Hall, 1996. Accessible and engaging text covering traditional areas of criminology as well as questions of popular concern and contemporary police debate.

McAlary, Mike. *Good Cop Bad Cop: Detective Joe Trimboli's Heroic Pursuit of NYPD Officer Michael Dowd.* New York: Pocket Books, 1994. Award-winning *New York Daily News* journalist delivers a riveting account of the biggest police scandal to rock New York in 25 years.

Miller, Charly D., and Bryan E. Brady. *EMT-Paramedic National Standards Review Self Test.* 3rd ed. Indianapolis: Brady, 1997. An excellent guide to preparing for the standard exam.

Moore, Alvin Edward. *Border Patrol.* Santa Fe: Sunstone Press, 1997. An insightful and informative overview of the profession, including a detailed history of immigration in the United States.

O'Neill, Hugh E., Hy Hammer, and E. P. Steinberg. *Police Officer.* 13th ed. New York: Arco Publishers, 1997. A classic guide, offering up-to-the-minute coverage of police officer qualifying tests all over America. Includes five full-length sample exams.

Phillips, David Atlee. *Careers in Secret Operations: How to Be a Federal Intelligence Officer.* Bethesda: University Publications of America, 1985. Offers excellent vocational guidance on various intelligence occupations within various intelligence agencies.

Pistone, Joseph D., with Richard Woodley. *Donnie Brasco: My Undercover Life in the Mafia.* New York: Signet, 1997. The book on which the well-known movie was based. An unforgettable account of how an undercover FBI agent became a part of the mysterious, deadly world of the mafia he was trained to expose.

Powers, Tyrone. *Eyes to My Soul: The Rise or Decline of a Black FBI Agent.* Dover: Majority Press, 1996. An excellent first-hand account of the—sometimes deeply disturbing—difficulties faced by African American FBI agents.

Schroeder, Donald J., and Frank A. Lombardo. *How to Prepare for the Correction Officer Examination.* Hauppauge: Barrons Educational Series, 1996. A useful study guide to the exam that also offers insight into what a corrections officer can expect after passing it.

Schroeder, Donald J. and Frank A. Lombardo. How *to Prepare for the Police Officer Examination.* 4th ed. Hauppauge: Barrons Educational Series, 1992. Essential reading for anyone who aspires to a police career; presents general information, strategies for achieving a high score on competitive police exams, and four full-length exams.

Shelby, Philip. *Days of Drums: A Novel.* New York: Simon & Schuster, 1996. A compelling novel about one of four women who works in Executive Protection, assigned to guard a controversial senator.

Steinberg, Eve P. *Correction Officer.* 11th ed. New York: Arco Publishers, 1997. The first choice of correction officers for more than 40 years, this thorough book is filled with valuable and current information about test-taking practice. Includes sample exams, detailed explanations, and illustrations.

Stoy, Walt A. *Mosby's EMT: Basic Textbook.* St. Louis: Mosby-Year-Book, 1995. Comprehensively discussed and illustrated guide to the core material of the revised EMT basic curriculum, as outlined by the U.S. Department of Transportation.

Swearingen, M. Wesley. *FBI Secrets: An Agent's Expose.* Somerville: South End Press, 1995. A former FBI agent exposes the agency's fallacies and wars against political freedom in this country, telling of intrigue, sanctioned murder, and perjury. A fascinating book, and a must-read for anyone interested in secret agency activities.

PERIODICALS

Arrest Law Bulletin. Published monthly by the Quinlan Publishing Co., 23 Drydock Avenue, Boston, MA 02210. Sheds light on what does and does not constitute a lawful arrest, through court cases that cover such issues as probable cause, warrantless arrests, and investigative stops.

Border Patrol Web Site. Updated regularly by the United States Border Patrol at http://members.aol.com. Offers news, photographs, special articles and reports, information about training requirements and job opportunities, and links to other immigration and law enforcement sites.

Center for the Study of Intelligence Newsletter. Published bi-annually by the Center for the Study of Intelligence, Central Intelligence Agency, Washington, DC, 20505. Addresses theoretical, practical, and historical intelligence issues. Often publishes interesting declassified documents, information about upcoming seminars, and announcements concerning academic developments within intelligence.

Civil Rights Journal. Published monthly by the U.S. Civil Rights Commission Publications Office, 624 Ninth Street, NW, Washington, DC 20425. An important journal that calls attention to incidents of harassment, brutality, intimidation, and other infringements on people's rights, particularly in law enforcement.

Criminal Victimization. Published yearly by the Bureau of Justice Statistics, U.S. Department of Justice, www.ojp.usdoj.gov/bjs. An indispensable statistical report summarizing criminal victimization rates and levels, including findings about the characteristics of victims.

Governing. Published monthly by Congressional Quarterly, Inc., 1414 22nd Street, NW, Washington, DC, 20037. A leading information source for state and local government that explains the inner machinations of law enforcement: how it works, what it costs, and why.

Jems: Journal of Emergency Medicine. Published monthly by Jems Communications, P.O. Box 2789, Carlsbad, CA 92018. A terrific journal for anyone interested in EMS careers, offering first-hand accounts from the field, special features about the daily lives of EMS workers, and articles about vehicles and equipment, medical developments, and innovations in emergency care.

Law Enforcement Bulletin. Published monthly by the Federal Bureau of Investigation, 935 Pennsylvania Avenue, NW, Washington, DC, 20035-0001. Produced and written by the agency, offering opinions, first-hand accounts from the field, special articles about developments in FBI training and practice, and job opportunities within various divisions.

Narcotics Law Bulletin. Published monthly by the Quinlan Publishing Co., 23 Drydock Avenue, Boston, MA 02210. Covers drug arrests and prosecutions; air surveillance, entrapment and other investigative tactics; informant-work; conspiracy theory; trafficking; and more.

Office of Correctional Education News. Published quarterly by the Office of Correctional Education, 600 Independence Avenue, SW, MES 4529, Washington, DC 20202-7242. Discusses and evaluates innovations in correctional education, and provides useful information on correctional research, history, and other federal and private resources available to practitioners serving incarcerated individuals.

On Patrol. Published quarterly by On Patrol Magazine, 116 West 8th Street, Suite 103, Georgetown, TX 78626. A premier law enforcement magazine that collects compelling stories about heroic police officers, and fascinating features on technology, justice, and society.

Police Department Disciplinary Bulletin. Published monthly by the Quinlan Publishing Co., 23 Drydock Avenue, Boston, MA 02210. Articles discussing the when and how of disciplining officers, avoiding disciplinary problems, and related subjects.

The Police Officer's Internet Directory. Updated daily at http://www.officer.com. An extremely useful Web site, assembling various links to law enforcement agencies, employment bulletins, special ops, training events, and many other police resources.

10/75. Updated daily at http://www.10-75.com. An excellent Web site for fire safety workers, offering up-to-date articles and news about rescue efforts, links to other fire safety sights, and key findings from various fire fighting studies.

VOMA. Published quarterly the Victim Offender Mediation Association (VOMA), c/o The Restorative Justice Institute, P.O. Box 16301, Washington, DC 20041-6301. An influential journal addressing basic concepts of victim-offender reconciliation, a now firmly established technique in criminal justice whereby criminals and victims resolve mutual hatred and tension through human, face-to-face contact.

Women Police. Published quarterly by the International Association of Women Police, North Deer Isle Road, Box 149, Deer Isle, ME 04627-9700. A journal produced by a fast-growing, dynamic organization that addresses the concerns of women in various areas of police or law enforcement work.

Ask for Money

FIRST

By the time most students get around to thinking about applying for scholarships, they have already extolled their personal and academic virtues to such lengths in essays and interviews for college applications that even their own grandmothers wouldn't recognize them. The thought of filling out yet another application form fills students with dread. And why bother? Won't the same five or six kids who have been fighting over grade point averages since the fifth grade walk away with all the really *good* scholarships?

The truth is, most of the scholarships available to high school and college students are being offered because an organization wants to promote interest in a particular field, encourage more students to become qualified to enter it, and finally, to help those students afford an education. Certainly, having a good grade point average is a valuable asset, and many organizations who grant scholarships request that only applicants with a minimum grade point average apply. More often than not, however, grade point averages aren't even mentioned; the focus is on the area of interest and what a student has done to distinguish himself or herself in that area. In fact, frequently the *only* requirement is that the scholarship applicant must be studying in a particular area.

GUIDELINES

When applying for scholarships, there are a few simple guidelines that can help ease the process considerably.

Plan Ahead
The absolute worst thing you can do is wait until the last minute. For one thing, obtaining recommendations or other supporting data in time to meet an application deadline is incredibly difficult. For another, no one does their best thinking or writing under the gun. So get off to a good start by reviewing schol-

arship applications as early as possible—months, even a year, in advance. If the current scholarship information isn't available, ask for a copy of last year's. Once you have the scholarship information or application in hand, give it a thorough read. Try to determine how your experience or situation best fits into the scholarship, or if it even fits at all. Don't waste your time applying for a scholarship in literature if you couldn't finish *Great Expectations*.

If possible, research the award or scholarship, including past recipients and, where applicable, the person in whose name the scholarship is offered. Often, scholarships are established to memorialize an individual who majored in religious studies or who loved history, for example, but in other cases, the scholarship is to memorialize the *work* of an individual. In those cases, try to get a feel for the spirit of the person's work. If you have any similar interests or experiences, don't hesitate to mention them.

Talk to others who received the scholarship, or to students currently studying in the area or field of interest in which the scholarship is offered, and try to gain insight into possible applications or work related to that field. When you're working on the essay asking why you want this scholarship, you'll have real answers: "I would benefit from receiving this scholarship because studying engineering will help me to design inexpensive but attractive and structurally sound urban housing."

Take your time writing the essays. Be certain you are answering the question or questions on the application and not merely restating facts about yourself. Don't be afraid to get creative; try to imagine what you would think of if you had to sift through hundreds of applications. What would you want to know about the candidate? What would convince you that someone was deserving of the scholarship? Work through several drafts and have someone whose advice you respect—a parent, teacher, or guidance counselor—review the essay for grammar and content.

Finally, if you know in advance which scholarships you want to apply for, there might still be time to stack the deck in your favor by getting an internship, volunteering, or working part-time. Bottom line: the more you know about a scholarship and the sooner you learn it, the better.

Follow Directions

Think of it this way: many of the organizations that offer scholarships devote 99.9 percent of their time to something other than the scholarship for which you are applying. Don't make a nuisance of yourself by pestering them for information. Simply follow the directions you are given. If the scholarship information specifies that you should write for information, then write for it— don't call.

Pay close attention to whether you're applying for an award, a scholarship, a prize, or financial aid. Often these words are used interchangeably, but just as often they have different meanings. An award is usually given for something you have done: built a park or helped distribute meals to the elderly; or something you have created: a design, an essay, a short film, a screenplay, an invention. On the other hand, a scholarship is frequently a renewable sum of money that is given to a person to help defray the costs of college. Scholarships are given to candidates who meet the necessary criteria based on essays, eligibility, grades, or sometimes all three.

Supply all the necessary documents, information, and fees, and make the deadlines. You won't win any scholarships by forgetting to include a recommendation from your teacher or failing to postmark the application by the deadline. Bottom line: get it right the first time, on time.

Apply Early

Once you have the application in hand, don't dawdle. If you've requested it far enough in advance, there shouldn't be any reason for you not to turn it in well in advance of the deadline. You never know, if it comes down to two candidates, your timeliness just might be the deciding factor. Bottom line: don't wait, don't hesitate.

Be Yourself

Don't make promises you can't keep. There are plenty of hefty scholarships available, but if they all require you to study something that you don't enjoy, you'll be miserable in college. And the side effects from switching majors after you've accepted a scholarship could be even worse. Bottom line: be yourself.

Don't Limit Yourself

There are many sources for scholarships, beginning with your guidance counselor and ending with the Internet. All of the search engines have education categories. Start there and search by keywords, such as "financial aid," "scholarship," and "award." But don't be limited to the scholarships listed in these pages.

If you know of an organization related to or involved with the field of your choice, write a letter asking if they offer scholarships. If they don't offer scholarships, don't stop there. Write them another letter, or better yet, schedule a meeting with the president or someone in the public relations office and ask them if they would be willing to sponsor a scholarship for you. Of course, you'll need to prepare yourself well for such a meeting because you're selling a price-less commodity—yourself. Don't be shy, be confident. Tell them all about your-self, what you want to study and why, and let them know what you would be willing to do in exchange—volunteer at their favorite charity, write up reports on your progress in school, or work part-time on school breaks, full-time dur-ing the summer. Explain why you're a wise investment. Bottom line: the sky's the limit.

THE LIST

Alaska State Troopers
5700 East Tudor Road
Anchorage, AK 99507
Tel: 907-269-5611

The Michael Murphy Scholarship Fund provides loans of up to $1,000 per year for no more than six years to selected applicants who wish to pursue a certifi-cate or degree in law enforcement, probation, or a closely related area. To qual-ify, students must be accepted into or already studying at an accredited college, pursuing their studies full-time, and have lived in Alaska for at least two years immediately prior to application. To maintain their yearly awards and to have their awards renewed, certain standards of academic achievement and resi-dency requirements must be met. Recipients of this funding may repay it in cash or have one-fifth of the debt forgiven for each year they work in law enforcement in Alaska.

Alphonso Deal Scholarship
National Black Police Association
3251 Mount Pleasant Street, NW, Second Floor
Washington, DC 20010
Tel: 202-986-2070

The Alphonso Deal Scholarship Award is presented by the National Black Police Association to a high school senior who wishes to study law enforce-ment or a closely related field at a two- or four-year college. Applicants must be U.S. citizens and accepted into their college of choice. The scholarship is awarded on the basis of academic achievement, recommendations, and char-acter. The amount of the award is at the discretion of the National Black Police Association's Scholarship Committee.

American Police Hall of Fame Educational Scholarship Fund
American Police Hall of Fame and Museum
3801 Biscayne Boulevard
Miami, FL 33137
Tel: 305-573-0070

To provide financial assistance for college education to children of deceased or disabled law enforcement officers. Applicants must be immediate family members of law enforcement officers killed, permanently injured, or disabled in the line of duty. Awards depend on the availability of funds and the number of recipients, but are at least $1,000.

ASCLD Scholarship Awards
American Society of Crime Laboratory Directors
Attn: Education and Training Committee
c/o Niagara County Sheriff's Department Forensic Laboratory
5526 Niagara Street
PO Box 496
Lockport, NY 14094
Tel: 716-439-9360

Applicants must be full-time undergraduate or graduate students in a forensic science program recognized by the American Society of Crime Laboratory Directors and planning a career in forensic science. They must maintain an overall GPA of at least 3.0. Selection is not based on financial need, but on scholastic and forensic records, personal statements, and faculty recommendations. There are two awards of up to $1,000 given every year.

Cooperative Education Program of the National Security Agency
National Security Agency M3222
Fort Meade, MD 20755-6000
Tel: 410-859-4590

Applicants for this program must be U.S. citizens enrolled in the cooperative education program at their college or university with a GPA of at least 3.0. They must be studying engineering (with an emphasis on electronic communications systems), computer science, or languages (Asian, Middle Eastern, or Slavic). A background investigation is required. Students normally apply at the end of the freshman year and begin their first work tour after completion of the sophomore year. Salaries are based on the percentage of credits completed toward a degree, starting at $18,257 per year and increasing for each twenty percent block of credits completed until the maximum of $25,061 per year is reached. Participants are eligible for all benefits of permanent employees. Students are also eligible to apply for tuition reimbursement while working.

Hanly Scholarship
Association of Former Agents of the U.S. Secret Service
PO Box 11681
Alexandria, VA 22312

Open to college juniors and seniors; applicants must have completed at least one year of study in law enforcement and must be U.S. citizens. Selection is based upon academic standing. Awarded every year. The amount of each award and the total number of awards vary each year.

J. Clifford Dietrich Scholarship
Association of Former Agents of the U.S. Secret Service
PO Box 11681
Alexandria, VA 22312

Open to college juniors and seniors; applicants must have completed at least one year of study in law enforcement and must be U.S. citizens. Selection is based upon academic standing. Awarded every year. The award is between $500 and $2,000; the number of scholarships available varies.

J. Edgar Hoover Foundation Scholarship
Boy Scouts of America
1325 Walnut Hill Lane
Irving, TX 75038
Tel: 214-580-2433

Applicants must be high school seniors who are active and registered members of a law enforcement Explorer post. The award is $1,500; the number of scholarships available varies.

John Charles Wilson Scholarships
International Association of Arson Investigators
PO Box 91119
Louisville PO, KY 40291
Tel: 502-491-7482

Undergraduate college students currently studying or planning to study police or fire science are eligible for these scholarships. Applicants must be members of IAAI, relatives of IAAI members, or sponsored or recommended by members. Three awards are given annually in amounts determined by the Scholarship Committee.

Julie Y. Cross Scholarship
Association of Former Agents of the U.S. Secret Service
PO Box 11681
Alexandria, VA 22312

Open to college juniors and seniors; applicants must have completed at least one year of study in law enforcement and must be U.S. citizens. Selection is based upon academic standing. Awarded every year. The award is between $500 and $2,000; the number of scholarships available varies.

Law Enforcement Assistance Award
Boy Scouts of America
1325 West Walnut Hill Lane
PO Box 152079
Irving, TX 75015-2079
Tel: 214-580-2000

This program is open to Explorer Scouts who assist law enforcement agencies with meaningful and exceptional service. Candidates must have performed "an act which assisted in the prevention or solution of a serious crime or an act which assisted in leading to the apprehension of a felony suspect wanted by a law enforcement agency." They must be active members of a law enforcement Explorer post currently registered with the Boy Scouts of America. This award consists of a framed certificate, a $1,000 scholarship, an engraved medallion, and a special lapel pin.

Law Enforcement Explorer Scholarships
U.S. Customs Service
1301 Constitution Avenue, Room 3422
Washington, DC 20229
Tel: 202-927-6724

Scholarships are open to high school seniors or college students who are registered Explorer Scouts active in a law enforcement post. An essay and letters of recommendation are required. The stipend is $1,000. Funds are paid directly to the recipients' schools.

Lt. Gen. Eugene F. Tighe, Jr., USAF Memorial Scholarship
Association of Former Intelligence Officers
San Diego Chapter
13785 Quinton Road
San Diego, CA 92129

Based on academic achievement; minimum GPA required is 3.0. Applicants must be studying or planning to study criminal justice. An essay is required as part of the application.

Public Service Scholarship
Public Employees Roundtable
PO Box 6184, Ben Franklin Station
Washington, DC 20044-6184
Tel: 202-927-5000

Applicants must be studying or intending to study public service and planning a career in public service at the local, state, or federal level. Include a SASE with your request for information and your application. Selection is based on your career goals and essay. There are between eight and twelve awards worth from $500 to $1,000 given every year.

Sheryl A. Horak Law Enforcement Explorer Memorial Scholarship
Boy Scouts of America
1325 Walnut Hill Lane
Irving, TX 75038
Tel: 214-580-2433

Scholarships are available to registered Explorer Scouts who are graduating high school seniors interested in pursuing a postsecondary degree in law enforcement. Scholarships are not renewable. Applications are available from your local Boy Scout chapter. The stipend is $1,000.

Special Agents Scholarships
Bureau of Alcohol, Tobacco, and Firearms
Liaison Program Manager
650 Massachusetts Avenue, Suite 7150
Washington, DC 20226
Tel: 202-927-777

Applicants must be studying or planning to study law enforcement. The stipend is $1,000. Funds are paid directly to the recipients' schools and may be used only for tuition.

Texas Sheriff's Association Scholarship

Southwest Texas State University
J. C. Kellam Building
San Marcos, TX 78666
Tel: 512-245-2340

Open to all college undergraduates; applicants must have at least a 2.5 GPA, have made a written commitment to a law enforcement career, and be eligible to serve as peace officers. Personal interview is required. There are two awards of $1,000 given every year.

Look to the Pros

The following professional organizations offer a variety of materials, from career brochures to lists of accredited schools to salary surveys. Many of them also publish journals and newsletters that you should become familiar with. Many also have annual conferences that you might be able to attend. (While you may not be able to attend a conference as a participant, it may be possible to cover one for your school or even your local paper, especially if your school has a related club.)

When contacting professional organizations, keep in mind that they all exist primarily to serve their members, be it through continuing education, professional licensure, political lobbying, or just keeping up with the profession. While many are strongly interested in promoting their profession and providing information about it to the general public, these professional organizations are busy with many other activities. Whether you call or write, be courteous, brief, and to the point. Know what you need and ask for it. If the organization has a Web site, check it out first: what you're looking for may be available there for downloading, or you may find a list of prices or instructions, such as sending a self-addressed stamped envelope with your request. Finally, be aware that organizations, like people, move. To save time when writing, first confirm the address, preferably with a quick phone call to the organization itself: "Hello, I'm calling to confirm your address. . . ."

THE SOURCES

The Alpha Group Center for Crime and Intelligence Analysis
PO Box 8
Montclair, CA 91763
Tel: 909-989-4366
Email: CrimeCrush@aol.com

Contact the Alpha Group for a schedule of courses in crime analysis, investigative analysis, and intelligence analysis throughout the United States and Canada. You can also get information about ordering a widely used textbook on crime analysis, *Crime Analysis: From First Report to Final Arrest,* by Steven Gottlieb.

The American Correctional Association
4380 Forbes Boulevard
Lanham, MD 20706
Tel: 301-918-1800
Web: http://www.corrections.com

Contact the ACA for information on job openings and for a list of universities that offer degree programs in corrections.

American Jail Association
2053 Day Road, Suite 100
Hagerstown, MD 21740
Tel: 301-790-3930
Email: AJA$Fred.net
Web: http://www.corrections.com/aja/index.html
Contact the AJA for information on careers in corrections.

American Society of Criminology
1314 Kinnear Road, Suite 212
Columbus, OH 43212
Tel: 614-292-9207
Web: http://www.bsos.umd.edu/asc/

Contact the ASC for information on careers in criminology.

Association of Former Intelligence Officers
6723 Whittier Avenue, Suite 303A
McLean, VA 22101
Tel: 703-790-0320

Contact the AFIO for information about careers in intelligence, their student essay contest, and a list of members willing to speak at schools.

The Federal Bureau of Investigation
Personnel Resources Office
J. Edgar Hoover FBI Building
Tenth Street and Pennsylvania Avenue, NW
Washington, DC 20535
Tel: 202-324-3000
Web: http://www.fbi.gov

Contact the FBI for information on a career as an FBI agent.

Federal Bureau of Prisons
National Recruitment Office
320 First Street, NW, Room 460
Washington, DC 20534
Web: http://www.bop.gov

Contact the FBP for information on entrance requirements, training, and career opportunities for corrections officers at the federal level.

Federal Investigators Association
2200 Wilson Boulevard
Box 102-219
Arlington, VA 22201

Contact the FIA for information about scholarships and careers in intelligence.

Immigration and Naturalization Service
425 I Street, NW
Washington, DC 20536
Tel: 202-514-2000
Web: http://www.ins.usdoj.gov

Go to the INS Web site for information about applying for employment with the INS, plus a list of frequently asked questions and answers. During open enrollment periods, call 912-757-3001, extension 960, to be sent information on testing. When the recruiting period is closed, call 202-616-1964 for recorded information on the next hiring period.

■ **International Association of Chiefs of Police**
515 North Washington Street
Alexandria, VA 22314
Tel: 703-836-6767
Web: http://www.theiacp.org/

Contact the IACP for information about careers in law enforcement.

■ **The International Association of Correctional Officers**
PO Box 81826
Lincoln, NE 68501
Tel: 800-255-2382 or 402-464-0602
Web: http://www.acsp.uic.edu/iaco

Contact the IACO for information on a career as a corrections officer.

■ **International Association of Crime Analysts**
PO Box 937
Arvada, CO 80001
Web: http://web2.airmail.net/iaca

IACA offers a list of members who are available for peer support and assistance in solving problems as well as a quarterly newsletter with a forum for asking questions. At their Web site, you'll find a partial membership roster, information about the annual meeting, and links to other criminal justice sites.

■ **International Association of Fire Chiefs**
4025 Fair Ridge Drive
Fairfax, VA 22033-2868
Tel: 703-273-0911
Web: http://www.iafc.org

IAFC offers information on scholarships, employment, and job preparation.

■ **International Association of Firefighters**
1750 New York Avenue, NW
Washington, DC 20006
Tel: 202-737-8484
Web: http://www.iaff.org

IAFF offers information about becoming a professional firefighter, including the duties, working conditions, and salary and benefits.

National Association of Emergency Medical Technicians
102 West Leake Street
Clinton, MS 39056
Tel: 800-346-2368
Web: http://www.naemt.org

Contact NAEMT for information about a career as an emergency medical technician.

National Fire Protection Association
One Batterymarch Park
PO Box 9101
Quincy, MA 02269-9101
Tel: 617-770-3000
Web: http://www.nfpa.org/

NFPA offers information about professional firefighter qualifications and a list of colleges and universities that offer two- or four-year college degree programs in fire science or fire prevention.

National Sheriffs' Association
1450 Duke Street
Alexandria, VA 22314-3490
Tel: 800-424-7827
Web: http://www.sheriffs.org/

Contact the NSA for information on careers in law enforcement and corrections.

Society of Fire Protection Engineers
One Liberty Square
Boston, MA 02109-4825
Tel: 617-482-0686
Web: http://www.wpi.edu.Academics/Depts/Fire/SFPE/

SFPE offers information on student research grants and student chapters of the Society of Fire Protection Engineers.

U.S. Fire Administration
16825 South Seton Avenue
Emmitsburg, MD 21727
Tel: 301-447-1000
Web: http://www.usfa.fema.gov/

USFA offers information about national fire programs, statistics on fire fighting, and details about the National Fire Academy.

U.S. Office of Personnel Management
Career America Connection Line
Theodore Roosevelt Federal Building
1900 E Street, NW, Room 1416
Washington, DC 20415-0001
Web: http://www.usajobs.opm.gov/a.htm

At this user-friendly Web site, you can search for current job openings with the Border Patrol.

Index